# What's On My

# Mind?

# Coping Takes Work

## VOLUME II

Edited by Sarah Mayor

Ashley Smith

Contributors: Brian Anderson, Terresa Ford, Pat Strode,
Shannon Murphy, Stacey Walker, Sr.

**Publisher's Note:** This read is not a substitute for medical advice. Continue to seek an official diagnosis and treatment recommendations from mental health professionals. The reader should regularly consult with their physician about health needs.

# DEDICATION

I dedicate *Coping Takes Work* to my network of support. I appreciate each of you for your understanding, support, and love. To my family and friends. Also, to my psychiatrist and therapists over the years, I appreciate your commitment to medicine and service to clients. *Coping Takes Work* is my gift, message, and thanks to God, and humanity. My support system is priceless, and so is my journey of recovery.

Much love,

Ashley.

"It's not the load that breaks you down, it's the way you carry it."

–Lena Horne

# Author's Note

This book focuses on practical coping tools to master resiliency. Medication is commonly viewed as a vital means to practice recovery. My recovery demands more than medication, it requires hard work. This is my story.

I established my blog, *Overcoming Schizophrenia,* in 2008. The blog details my experience with mental illness. My first book, *What's On My Mind? Volume I* is a collection of blog entries from *Overcoming Schizophrenia.* Accordingly, *Coping Takes Work* is a continuation of volume I with blog entries dating from 2014-2019. I edited and remastered parts of these blog articles.

Even though this book is for peers in recovery, it is also a great resource for mental health professionals, caregivers, and others. I am not a doctor, and this book will not discuss specific medications. However, I have a wealth of knowledge about recovery based on personal experience that will be an asset to newly diagnosed peers and individuals who are more familiar with recovery over time.

I encourage you to take notes. Also, share this book with others to overcome stigma and to support persons in recovery. Welcome to my recovery world.

Ashley Smith

# CONTENTS

# ACKNOWLEDGMENTS

First, I give all credit to The Creator for this life and experience. I am nothing without The One. I thank God for allowing me to share my recovery story and offer hope to those facing similar challenges.

I give special recognition to my family for their unconditional love and support: Ali, Tanya Anderson, Belinda Cullins, Big Boy, Allen Ford, Kira and Jerome Ford, Bridgette France, Clarence Gulley, Demetrius Gulley, Rita Hicks, Paul Lewis, Sr., Erica Quarles, Olyc Quarles, Tina Quarles-Gulley, Christina Thorpe Rogers, Carlys Smith, J.B. Smith, Rachel Smith, Valyncia Smith, Rodney Strickland, Relatives of the Thirkield Family, Julia Triplett, Sydney Triplett, and Zora.

There are many individuals who have supported my advocacy work and recovery. I thank each of you: Brian Anderson, Sally Atwell, Steve Ayer, Christina Bacopoulos, Liz Barten, Selina Beene, Joshua Bell, Terrell Blalock, Angela Brathwaite, Alfred Brooks, Sr., Christina Bruni, Donna Bullard, Cassandra Byrd, Marcus Carter, James Clint Chapman, Jacqlyn Charles, Cathryn Coone-McCrary, Jake Curtis, Kay DeMott, Karen Demski, Jean Dervan, Erica Duncan, Carlos Eady, Melody Favor, Terresa Ford, Martee Horne, Annie Hunter, Hadassah Israel, Tonya Jenkins, Corey Jones, Kim

Jones, Nicole Evans Jones, Doreen Kennie, Shalette Lawton, Gregory Lunceford, Janey Lyons, Mimi Marlowe, Sarah Mayor, Carol McEntee, Carlton Michael, Shayne Moore, Susan Gail Bryan Morgan, Terri Morgan, Shannon Murphy, Greg Panico, Rebecca Phillips, Nzingha Rahni, Christal Reynolds, Andrew Samuels, Robert Sanders, Pamela Shulterbrandt, Joel Slack, Bobbie Slocumb, Eric Spencer, Pat Strode, Faye Taylor, Gloria Thomas, Jean Toole, Jonathan Tucker, Stephanie Tyree, Tamika Vasser, Phoebe Sparrow Wagner, Stacey Walker, Sr., Valerie West, Karl Lorenz Willett, Bethany Yeiser.

Lastly, I thank the following organizations and groups:

Community Friendship, Inc.

CURESZ Foundation

Embracing My Mind, Inc. Facebook Page Fans

EMM Enterprise, LLC

Emory University School of Medicine

Hope through Divine Intervention, Inc.

Janssen Pharmaceuticals, Inc.

NAMI Georgia, Inc.

The Overcoming Schizophrenia Blog Readers

The Respect Institute of Georgia

# STATEMENT OF SUPPORT

"Over the last ten years, Ashley has worked with Hope through Divine Intervention, Inc. demonstrating her abilities to live a quality, functional life while offering support to others who have experienced the same challenges. She gives hope that they too can live a "normal" life in recovery. Through her experience she has been able to have a dramatic impact on the lives of others. She has given her time relentlessly to support individuals as well as herself to continue her journey. I witnessed her methods of service, and delivery, in helping others come to the realization that recovery is possible."

**–Selina Beene, Co-Founder of Hope through Divine Intervention, Inc.**

# STATEMENT OF SUPPORT

"Ms. Ashley Smith has learned to live with and overcome symptoms of schizophrenia and gone on to have a full work and family life. She has become a vigorous advocate for those with severe mental illness, giving her time to the *National Alliance for the Mentally Ill,* becoming a certified peer specialist, and writing books to help those dealing with similar struggles. She has volunteered her time to be interviewed for course on *psychosis* for medical students at *Emory University.* Her frank, insightful, and inspiring comments about her experiences as a psychiatric patient have contributed deeply to their education on the meaning of recovery for those with severe mental illness."

**–Erica Duncan, MD, Attending Psychiatrist Atlanta VA Medical Center, and Professor Department of Psychiatry and Behavioral Sciences, Emory University School of Medicine**

# STATEMENT OF SUPPORT

"Ashley Smith's body of work regarding recovery from mental health challenges is insightful based on her own journey and deep empathy for others. Most of all, it is practical, and based on the realities of what it is like to grapple with a mental health crisis. Her writing provides the guidance to get better, step by step. Ashley is a great resource for the mental health community and a wonderful collaborator for mental health education projects."

**–Greg Panico, Retired Communications Leader for Janssen Pharmaceuticals, and Lifelong Health Educator**

# PREFACE

In 2008, I started blogging about my schizophrenia. In the beginning, I blogged anonymously. There is a lot of stigma around mental illness. However, I learned a lot about recovery through peer support, enabling me to gain insight into a world that is highly stigmatized and struggle to understand mental illness as a society at large. As I acquired a wealth of information on recovery, I gained more self-confidence and made a conscious decision to disclose my diagnosis to the world. Despite the stigma that plagues my condition, I attached my real name to the blog, *Overcoming Schizophrenia.*

*What's On My Mind? Volume I* is a collection of blog entries from *Overcoming Schizophrenia.* This book details the beginning of my diagnosis, which came about through a legal incident in 2007. My undiagnosed mental illness created turmoil in my mind that unfortunately led to legal ramifications, but also helpful interventions. In spite of these setbacks, I rediscovered myself and fought back against the odds.

Still, the fight continues for my wellness, stability, and position as a mental health advocate. The fight against the stigma of mental illness tries to bring me down. Therefore, I use my blog as an advocacy weapon, sharing my testimony to change perspectives. Also, to reduce widespread negative connotations that aim to attack our identity, character, and that threatens our unique wellbeing.

I have a firm foundation in recovery through my family, peers, and faith in God. I developed inner strength from my support system and acquired a vision of hope. I credit my state hospital doctor who diagnosed me, and my mother for instilling my optimistic views on recovery, which persists to my present-day outlook.

As mentioned in *What's On My Mind? Volume I,* sharing my testimony was only the beginning. Accordingly, *What's On My Mind? Coping Takes Work, Volume II,* is an update on my life with schizophrenia. However, *Coping Takes Work* brings emphasizes to my determination to bounce back from hospitalization and to stay in a good place mentally, emotionally, spiritually, and physically.

In 2018, I was hospitalized - but not crushed. This was my second hospitalization, occurring 11 years after diagnosis. I reclaimed control of my life by applying the many lessons I learned regarding coping skills. Hospitalization may be unavoidable for people with my diagnosis or similar conditions. Fortunately, resiliency is a part of the recovery lifestyle.

This book focuses on my transformation in recovery from the last few years, 2014-2019. However, most blog entries bring attention to how I bounced back after the hospitalization. I channel in on practical coping strategies that I used to get well. Throughout this read, I focus on two objectives:

1. Therapy is a crucial coping tool for recovery, and

2. Redefining recovery by practices geared toward keeping in a good place.

## Education and Training

I have a background in business administration and psychology. I attended Oglethorpe University in Atlanta, Georgia, for three years. My major was business administration. I went to Southwestern College in Chula Vista, California, for business administration. When I returned to Atlanta, I attended Georgia State University and studied psychology. I have an extensive background in mental health through first-hand experience and advocacy. I learned how to model recovery by receiving and giving peer support. I facilitated support groups and articulated anti-stigma messages through different projects.

In 2007, my recovery journey started with legal interventions. I learned of my diagnosis through an unfortunate incident that involved a high-speed chase with police. This was the result of my mind wars to escape the demons that I feared, which outnumbered me and aimed to kill me. I received court-enforced treatment in jail and the state psychiatric hospital. Details of my symptoms, experience, and approaches to mental health awareness projects are portrayed in *What's On Mind? Volume I.*

After the incident, I joined a housing program and clubhouse for young adults living with mental health conditions. The clubhouse offered Mary Ellen Copeland's Wellness Recovery Action Plan (WRAP) classes focusing on recovery and crisis planning. The facilitator had a diagnosis like mine, which inspired me to coordinate classes and to offer peer support.

In 2009, I joined NAMI Georgia. The National Alliance on Mental Illness (NAMI) is the nation's largest grassroots non-profit organization providing mental health self-help groups and classes. They specialize in mental health programs for a variety of groups, such as veterans, teachers and parents, caregivers, families, and peers.

NAMI educated me on how to facilitate support groups. My leadership roles progressed from volunteer support group facilitator into the position of state trainer, and board member. I facilitated many classes, specifically for the program, In Our Own Voice. This program enables us to share our unique recovery stories. I trained peers on how to deliver the presentation for six years. I was a board member for NAMI Georgia from 2012 to 2014.

In 2009, I started a non-profit organization, Embracing My Mind (EMM). The organization's mission was to offer peer support by meeting the individual where they are on their recovery journey and sharing recovery tools to support self-sufficiency. I shared my recovery story and held group discussions about mental health challenges. Moreover, the objective of the classes was to enrich the understanding of recovery, to reduce self-stigma, and to instill hope among peers.

I learned about the Certified Peer Specialist (CPS) training through my therapist. The role of a CPS is to model recovery and to offer peer support, as well as maintaining ongoing education for counseling peers. In 2011, I participated in the CPS training that was facilitated by the Appalachian Consulting Group and the Georgia Mental Health Consumer Network (GMHCN).

In 2013, I became a trained speaker through the Respect Institute of Georgia, an arm of the Georgia Department of Behavioral Health and Developmental Disabilities. Respect Institute graduates learn how to articulate individual experiences of living in recovery. Our objectives were to destigmatize different disabilities, including physical and mental health challenges by discussing our personal experiences of setbacks, triumphs, and hopes.

## Lived Experience Expert

I am a lived experience expert on schizophrenia. A lived experience expert is an individual who has a first-hand account of various experiences related to the condition. My in-depth experience includes history with institutionalization, legal interventions, housing discrimination, therapy, disclosure, medication side effects, parenting a child while living in recovery, how to offer peer support, and conducting anti-stigma presentations and campaigns. I gained expertise through the CPS training, NAMI Georgia, Inc., and the Respect Institute of Georgia, along with numerous organizations. Moreover, my experience with challenges and hurdles in recovery speaks volumes on how to master resiliency.

Even though I was diagnosed with paranoid schizophrenia, my official diagnosis is schizoaffective disorder, bipolar type. I have been in recovery for over 12 years. Ever since I started this journey, I maintained one-on-one therapy sessions that help me manage my health and life. I am a mother, peer, and mental health advocate; I am *not* a schizophrenic. I am a person living with schizophrenia and bipolar disorder. My name is Ashley Smith.

**What to Expect**

Every chapter opens with a statement that sets the tone. Select blog entries follow, and I conclude each chapter with a summary. Also, there are end of chapter self-reflection questions entitled: "My Self-Care Journal."

The "Introduction" and "Final Words," chapters do not include any blog articles, nor end of chapter questions. You will find Appendix A, B, C, D, E, F, and G to be full of recovery stories and letters to our caregivers and therapists. These stories offer a different perspective on how to master wellness in spite of the impact that mental health challenges have on our lives.

Appendix A, B, and C were written by peers in recovery. Brian Anderson is a Certified Peer Specialist (CPS) and the author of *Beautiful Scars: My Journey to Wholeness and Healing,* and *Beautiful Scars, Two: The Ripple Effect.* Terresa

Ford is a CPS and Hearing Voices Network facilitator. Currently, she enriches her education in the study of a Master of Divinity. Stacey Walker, Sr. is an army veteran, CPS, and author of *Principles of Biblical Leadership: Identity of a Leader.* Each of these individuals provide us with a glimpse into their world of recovery and how they manage life.

Pat Strode is a caregiver. Her story and coping strategy can be found in Appendix D. She provides insight into the hope of a caregiver who experiences the recovery journey with us. Pat is an Advocate Coordinator for the Georgia Crisis Intervention Team (CIT), and secretary of CIT International, Inc. Appendix E is my letter to my caregiver: my stepfather. In this letter, I offer tips to caregivers based on my relationship with mine.

Appendix F is a letter by my former therapist, Shannon Murphy, LPC, CPCS. Shannon's letter addresses her colleagues within the work of conducting therapy sessions. In 2018, Shannon helped me bounce back after my hospitalization. Shannon's letter is important to add to this work because it embodies a pivotal profession that empowers us and should be recognized as a model for all professionals in the mental health field. I value all of the mental health professionals I worked with over the years. Their expertise strengthened my foundation in recovery and positive outcomes.

Appendix G is my story about my son, Big Boy, and my struggle to be a good parent in the midst of the challenges accompanying my illness.

I have known the contributing authors for a few years; we are fighting the same war against stigma. We strive to uphold balance and wellness by our lifestyles. Our stories are the advocacy weapons to overcome the stigma of mental illness, but also to empower ourselves and each other. We have different stories and use our coping skills to live quality lives in recovery. The Appendixes are a tremendous asset to this read, providing diverse perspectives on the recovery journey.

The "Links and Resources," page will direct you to helpful schizophrenia information and related websites. There are several advantages to therapy that I share throughout this book. I hope that you will feel inspired to keep trying to stay in your good place by practicing the coping techniques that work well for you. Also, if you do not have a therapist, I encourage you to seek therapy as an additional coping tool. Thank you.

# INTRODUCTION

An individual living with schizophrenia, or any mental illness, must continue to endure. The reward is recovery and your life. (*What's On My Mind? Volume I,* "Final Words").

---

Before my diagnosis I identified with most people of my age and held on to many hopes for my future. When I was a child I wanted to sing, and dance like famous female artist. When I was a teenager, I hoped to live the American dream within ten years, graduating from a great institution, marrying a rich man, having kids, and excelling in my career.

Moreover, I came from a hard-working family, listened to popular music, and attended school. None of my hopes, and dreams included a life-altering event such as mental illness. In fact, I did not understand schizophrenia before my diagnosis. In general, society holds many negative ideas about my diagnosis of schizophrenia and bipolar disorder; accordingly, people do not aim to relate to individuals with such health concerns. They often wrongfully judge us.

1

My goal is to share awareness, hope, and understanding for not only myself but also for my peers in recovery. Peers have goals, families, and purpose. Despite my diagnosis, a lot of people played intricate roles in helping me connect with resources, redirecting my focus, and regaining the girl I was - into the woman I am still becoming. Among my treatment team, family, and peers, my mother was my anchor. In fact, my mother told me she could see me sharing with others about how I made it through [my schizophrenia], and I believed her...

I could not be the woman I aspire to be to my loved ones, peers, and to the world without my mother, Tina Quarles-Gulley. She is no longer here in the flesh; however, I am committed to living her vision of my recovery, which is now my life's purpose: mental health advocacy. Being in recovery over 12 years instills many vital lessons on how to love unconditionally, and especially how to persevere, practicing wellness for my recovery, and livelihood.

**Superwoman**

The woman who gave life to me was in every sense of the word a mother. She was not my girlfriend, nor the laid-back type; my mother was strict, reinforced structure, and loved our family dearly. "I love you," were the words we departed on. She never tolerated me nor my sister, Valyncia, to call each other, "stupid," nor down-talk. My mother called me her "little raccoon," "princess," and "pretty girl."

One of my favorite childhood memories was our Saturday routine. Every Saturday morning, I beat my sister to the television, and watched the cartoon line-up. Our mother cooked pancakes, making mine look like a "Mickey Mouse" face. After breakfast my mother started the music and we would dance and clean. The music was always the same with a combination of classic oldies and legendary singers including: The Temptations, Diana Ross and the Supremes, Donna Summers, Whitney Houston, Betty Wright, and Karyn White. Cleaning our apartment was fun, we would sing and dance to the rhythms, especially, "Poppa Was a Rolling Stone."

The man who raised me, my stepfather, Clarence Gulley, came into our lives when I was seven years old. He was a native of San Francisco and worked as an electrician. My parents developed diverse business ventures that focused on construction, antiques, and online business. They were together for over 20 years until my mother's passing in 2013. My sister and I called mom, "superwoman," because she always made-it-happen!

Prior to her marriage to my stepfather, my mother worked a lot and had high expectations for my sister and I in terms of education and behavior, evidenced by correcting our speech, expecting us to complete homework and chores immediately after school – if we wanted to have any fun! From grade school onward I participated in a range of extracurricular activities including gymnastics, basketball, volleyball, track and field, cross country, and clubs such as Students Against Destructive Decisions (SADD), Parent Teacher Student Association (PTSA), the school drama club, and choir. I excelled academically and went to the four-year private liberal arts institution where my sister graduated with her undergraduate degree in Atlanta.

After completing three years at the university, I took a break from school in March 2007. It was one of the most discouraging days of my life. I slipped notes underneath the doors of my professors and said my goodbyes. As I walked off the campus, I felt a huge black cloud hover over me on that bright day, and I dared not look back at the site of the school which had been my life - and represented my failed dreams. My coach emailed me and asked me if I needed a scholarship, but I lost my motivation and desire to finish my academic race, a race I had worked very hard for from day one.

I made the Dean's List my freshmen year, completed two internships, and was a student aide to my professor. Within a couple of days, I was on a flight back to California where I was raised until the age of 12. I moved to southern California to live and work with my aunt, and in order to regroup with plans to return to school.

However, my mind started playing tricks on me that I had never experienced before. My mind could not maintain life's stresses: taking a break from school, relocating from Georgia back to California, and starting a new life with relatives other than my immediate family. Ultimately, it was hard to manage these transitions quickly, which worsened my undiagnosed mental health condition.

By June 2007, three short months of transition, I was jailed and hospitalized for five months with pending felony charges. This milestone changed my life goals, lifestyle, and medical history forever. Ultimately, my experience challenged all of me, making me love stronger, work harder, and build resiliency. I had to let go of the old Ashley in order to begin developing the new Ashley.

In short, I had to accept my medical condition, adopt other people's vision of my recovery, and work on a new unimaginable life mission. My plan was to excel and to live a fulfilling life despite mental illness in order to share my experience and empower others through example, advocacy, and passion for the recovery movement. To do this, I had to put myself out there.

My medical setback was more than an individual concern, it was a family crisis. Being diagnosed with a medical condition such as schizophrenia challenged my entire family; emotionally, financially, and spiritually. This pushed limits beyond just those of my immediate family, but empowered us all, despite the many aspects of social challenges and discrimination.

## Losing Ashley

My undiagnosed symptoms of schizophrenia involved a realm of unthinkable senses, altered realities, and fears. The unknown symptoms kidnapped my mind for a merry-go-round of mental turmoil. Where my mind took me, nobody was allowed. I couldn't trust anyone - not family, nor friends, not even my own mother, who loved me unconditionally. Everybody was a threat! I felt like they were imposters pretending to be members of my family. Eventually, my reality was fading, life was intense, and my sanity was unknowingly deteriorating. I became alone, scared, and the world's most sought-after prey, at least in my mind.

Believing the world was out to get me was overwhelmingly frightening. It seemed as if everybody was obsessed with me and everywhere, I went, somebody was watching. Every comment I made somebody was listening. Every step I took somebody was monitoring. Street cameras zoomed in on me. I felt like the world was tuning into the same channel *watch* Ashley

Smith. *Get*, Ashley Smith. *Destroy*, Ashley Smith! I could not out-run them, everybody was in on it. I was outnumbered and under attack! My altered reality would not enable my mind to properly function or cope. I could not think clearly, making poor associations that didn't make sense – not even to me. Yet, my mind told me to act (which I did) bizarrely and out of fear.

The day I was jailed was eerie, but then again so was I! I removed my eyeglasses and left my most prized possession; my Bible. My Bible was a gift from my church, and had my name engraved on it. My minister gave this gift to me upon my baptism at age 16 in September 2003, and I had carried it with me every day until then. I was 20 years old. I ditched my cell phone because I thought I was being tracked. I almost trashed my purse but didn't - I needed my last cashed check from my job. At one point, I considered cutting off my dreadlocks, which I loved. I did these things to disguise myself, blend in, with hopes to escape with my life.

I was in a spiritual war zone. My gift of discernment disappeared. My ability to feel somebody's angelic nature versus their evilness was absent. Their mission to get me intensified - which horrified me. Overwhelmed with sensitivity, anxiety, and fear, I saw demons, lots of them. If an individual seemed to be glowing that meant they were "good," but if their eyes appeared black, they were "demonic." I made it to the airport but did not purchase the ticket. The woman behind the counter looked scary; she too had black eyes and appeared evil.

I accomplished an escape route that only God and I understood. Still, disoriented, hearing, and seeing things that nobody witnessed, I wanted help myself. I was fearful and in a daze. I strived to survive, and God knew my anguish and my heart, answering my unconscious prayers. I walked the grounds of the airport and into the parking lot. I quickly realized that somebody left their truck unattended because the driver's door was wide open with the keys in the ignition.

I wholeheartedly believed this truck was my miracle and transportation back home to Atlanta. In other words, I viewed a stranger's negligence, my place, and the timing as my only opportunity to escape the demons and a world that sought to harm me. In my mind, God had blessed me with a means to escape to safety, and I accepted.

I took the rugged unoccupied pickup truck from the parking lot and proceeded to the street. Seemingly within seconds of exiting the airport parking lot I heard sirens. I didn't think much of it because I did not have history with police. Besides, I was focused on survival at any cost. A train of police cars trailed my truck into the opposite flow of traffic and into a short-lived high-speed chase. I crashed the pickup truck into a building's wall in an effort to escape the police, who I thought were "in on it." My reality met the reality of bystanders: I was outnumbered by a force of police officers that surrounded and circled my crashed vehicle. With several guns pointed at me, instructions to surrender, and all I could concentrate on was my mission for God - which I did not thoroughly understand, but somehow, I believed I was Jesus Christ.

Out of fear for my life, I followed police orders, doing exactly as they instructed on loudspeaker, all while praying to God for a way out, and asking Him to forgive them. I was handcuffed, dreadfully frightened, but strong in my convictions. I recited the Lord's Prayer, asked God for His will to be done, and to let my mother and family know that I loved them. I believed the officers were demonic along with everyone else and planned to murder me (by explosion) in the back seat of the police car. They took me back to the airport police precinct. I was highly distressed and confused.

My family filed a missing person's report, and the investigator found me within a couple of days - in jail. My initial meeting with mom was eerie. When our eyes met, I could not distinguish the woman sitting on the other side of the window. Was she an imposter? I was cautious and afraid, because she *looked like mom*, but was different.

My eyes were glazed over, and my distant stare said it all; I was not well. I warned mom that if something happened to me, I did not commit suicide. With that said, she scurried away to meet my grandfather and a guard who were standing nearby. I knew something was wrong, but I could not reconcile the situation or understand the overall problems surrounding me.

When she sat back down in front of me, she appeared stressed out, fragile, and upset. To her, I must've looked worse! The way she looked at me alarmed me, as did my appearance to her. She told jail personnel I was anti-drugs, never used them. All of them just shut her down because they felt that they had heard it all before.

I was angered by her presence and that of our family. "I never want to see you again," I said without emotion. Detached, I walked away. I walked away with ease from the woman who gave me life. I denied all visitors, and trashed unopened mail from concerned relatives.

I became catatonic and would not move. Doctors asked me questions as they lifted my arm, "Does this hurt. Can you...?" Their presence and concerns did not stir me or ignite any response even though the visit was meant to help me. The symptoms smothered me, incapacitating my ability to advocate for myself.

I heard voices while the jail psychologist asked me about them. I did not engage him in his series of questioning because I did not trust him or connect in any way. In fact, he made me feel uncomfortable by his approach. He maintained a monotone voice, serious or limited facial expressions, and lacked any sense of rapport. Moreover, I thought the voices were my own estranged thoughts, which I could not sway, reduce, or control.

## Who Loves You?

The state hospital doctor adopted a scary diagnosis title for me, reducing my self-esteem. The new label discredited my academic successes, my community-focused involvement, and defined my confusion, character, and problem as being due to paranoid schizophrenia. Despite "old Ashley's rigorous background and commitments to church, community, and academic honors (Dean's List my freshmen year, a student mentor, a youth coach assistant, a cross country team runner for three years, a youth church leader, and many additional academic and community kudos) I would now be ostracized.

I was now reduced to being a schizophrenic, which meant no future for me. This diagnosis, a medical issue that I could not even see, became my new identity and position in society. The doctor's label for my condition instantly ingrained on my mind the ignorant beliefs and sentiments of society's disregard for people effected by mental illness.

Forced medication-compliance and classes about my diagnosis helped rekindle the old Ashley. I accepted family visits. Moreover, I accepted my life-long medical condition of paranoid schizophrenia; *something* had to explain why I had felony charges pending. *Something* explained my taking a military pickup truck, going on a high-speed chase with a fleet of police cars after me, and incurring major traffic violations.

I gave my treatment team permission to share medical information with my mom and family. Fortunately, my family met with my treatment team to learn more about my diagnosis, and to learn how to help me manage. Despite the wildfires racing across southern California, my doctor waited for my mother to have this important meeting about my condition and future care. In fact, he redirected her through back roads to the state hospital because of the significance of sharing information with my family, giving them important insights in terms of what to expect. My mother went through a list of questions that my stepfather and sister created together.

My doctor detailed potential side effects and identified the National Alliance on Mental Illness (NAMI) as a great support group for families.

Among the many questions and wealth of information discussed, my mother asked him what many families ask me to this day: What can family do - despite symptoms - to avoid losing their loved ones' trust? Those symptoms included: false beliefs, lack of trust, and delusions; and psychosis. My doctor replied, "Ask her, who loves you?"

## Negative Re-Play

There were many stressful events leading up to my second hospitalization. The weight of these situations overwhelmed my thoughts: my mother's fifth anniversary of her passing, a disruption in finances, moving into another house, and a breakdown within my support system. My setback was the accumulation of several weeks of excessive stress and lack of awareness of my drifting state of mind. The driving philosophy behind *mind over matter* did not apply when the severe symptoms of my diagnosis penetrated my thinking and ability to function.

These symptoms included: psychosis, paranoia, anxiety, delusions, and elevated energy. Psychosis is the lack of ability to distinguish reality from false beliefs and overinflated fears. Racing thoughts and confusion flooded my mind. My lack of sleep and high energy worsened my condition.

The root issue of my breakdown and the severity of my brain disorder was the inability to function, to think clearly, and to uphold good judgment. How could I win an invisible battle? The malicious symptoms infiltrated my mind and my whole being, which manifested complete chaos; eventually, I realized I needed help.

## Mind Wars

The day started as usual, but in my mind, it never ended. One morning in August of 2018, I prepared my six-year-old son, Big Boy, for school. We walked to the neighborhood school bus stop and parted ways as usual with a hug and kiss. I thought I was fine because I had never stopped taking my medication, but I felt off-balanced. I was not myself. My thinking and normal thought-processing abilities could not understand my poor state of mind. In spite of the many warning signs and triggers that took place in the days before this event, I did not recognize my need for hospitalization.

A warning sign is an indication that my condition requires more attention. My warning signs included: lack of sleep, mania, a disruption in my routine, and high anxiety. Triggers are places, people, and events that worsen mental health problems and create issues with varying consequences – for example, financial hardship, grief, and crisis, etc.

Finally, on this day, I returned home and alerted my roommate that I needed to go to the hospital. My room portrayed the effects of a tornado, which was unlike me. I found a few items and packed light. I carried a tote bag with pictures of Big Boy, his blanket, and my journal. I had to focus on me and get well. It was time to check myself into the hospital.

I signed my name on the clipboard at the local psychiatric hospital and sat down in the empty lobby. The receptionist worsened my dread by requesting identification and my health insurance card; I did not have those with me. This paved the way for my mind to perpetuate conflicting ideas and to make a poor decision.

I changed my mind. I decided I would be okay and would not check myself into the hospital. I refused to sign the paperwork and walked away. I walked away from reason, thinking I could manage on my own. My delusions confused me, and psychosis set in. I was in and out of reality.

The problem was my thinking. My mind wars altered my judgment, took away my motivation to treat the root issue, and steadily led to my downfall. Denial, poor judgment, and confusion turned into my crisis. It was difficult to find clarity. My mind's war did not end, and my crisis began to spiral out of control.

That night I asked my stepfather, "Do you want me to go to the hospital? Yes, or no?" He replied, "Yes! I want you to go."

Thankfully, Big Boy was settled in with local family members. Though my stepfather lived in another state, the plan was for me to stay in the hospital in Atlanta. I spent the day in a daze as bystanders looked at me strangely, which added to the confusion.

My stepfather contacted the police so that they could escort me to the hospital. The officer's eyes were filled with compassion. I gave him my purse and sat in the back seat of the police car. When we arrived at the hospital, I insisted on admitting myself without assistance. Once again, I changed my mind. I walked out of the hospital doors for the second time that day. The plague of symptoms dominated my mind and worsened the situation.

At one point, I thought I was in a movie scene. It was the end of the world, and demons filled the parking lot. Suddenly, police lights surrounded me, and I was arrested. I shouted, pleading for them to let me go home. My high-energy, combined with the desire to return home, suffocated me. However, the door was shut while my mind's war marched on. It was an endless night.

Although my mind was fading, my spirit was still fighting. I began to question myself. Why was everybody looking at me, bizarrely? I felt off-balance but was still pressing forward. Was I some bizarre storm that caused others to see me differently? Was I hallucinating? I examined my face and body in the mirror of the jail cell. I peeled off the tips of my fingernails. Is this real? I wanted to escape out of my skin.

I contemplated moving to another place. I wanted to leave my family, country, and the world I knew, in order, to start over. I began to think of creating a new identity. I would change my name, relocate to another country, and start a new life, but *why*? Why?! Then a thought struck me, clarity overcame me, and finally, I gained insight.

My body started trembling, and I started crying profusely. I was frightened, but suddenly reconnected. Reality hit me. My mind was warring with itself, and I was the victim - but also the instigator! As I became unstuck, I had an epiphany. God told me what everybody else already knew.

My illness was at its worst, and my thinking was off-balance. My thoughts were spiraling out of control, adding to the turmoil. I was detrimentally unstable. I could not control my crisis, myself, nor my life at this point. I was losing myself, but I was the last to recognize the dominant indications of my poor state of mind.

My sporadic behavior and mood swings stalled intake processing at the jail. All I wanted was to stay in control. My crisis led to a forced hospitalization. I could not tell whether it was day or night, nor how long I had been jailed. To make matters worse, my mania would not permit much sleep - let alone allow my mind to calm itself and rest.

Then two officers arrived – it was time to go. They chained my hands and feet and escorted me to the van. The sun made my eyes feel sensitive, so I kept my head down as we walked. As the police escorted me to the psychiatric hospital, I was finally able to fall asleep. Thus, the ride was bumpy but short.

**The Intake Process**

When I arrived at the hospital, I was tired. I did not look up at anybody as we entered the intake unit. The staff was attentive and respectful. They speedily started processing me by taking a picture and guiding me into another room to change into a hospital gown. One by one, different nurses, therapists, case managers, and specialists met with me to gather information.

"My name is... please come with me. Do you know why you are here? Do you have a diagnosis? What medications do you take? When was the last time you had a tuberculosis shot? Do you have allergies?..."

"Hi, my name is... I will go over some paperwork with you. This form is on disclosure and confidentially. Please list your emergency contacts. Here is a copy of your patient's rights. Please sign here and don't forget this page right here. Wait here." ...Hi, my name is..."

My hospitalization in 2007 gave me an understanding of what to expect. Likewise, the intake process was long. I observed everybody and sought clues to familiarize myself with the rules. Generally, there are guidelines posted on the walls. I looked on the wall near the nurses' station and found a schedule.

The doctor holds the keys to everything. The doctor authorizes treatment, placement on units, expedited services, and requests. More importantly, they have the authority to order discharge processing. Therefore, I needed to know.

"When will I be able to see the doctor?" I asked.

"There are a few people ahead of you," the nurse replied. "They will call your name," she said.

There was a large seating area with a couple of small rooms to the side. There were plenty of areas to sit and to watch television. However, the tv created too much stimulation and sounded like noise to me. Most peers sat in the larger room, but I walked away and stayed in the hallway to seek solitude and silence. I appreciated the quietness away from everybody. Thankfully, the windows and natural sunlight were calming.

The hospital was a safe place. Peers did not judge each other. The staff was cordial and approachable. The hospital had a strict schedule that did not change unless there was a treatment team meeting. The treatment team meeting consisted of the doctor, therapist, nurse, and additional mental health professionals who discussed individualized treatment and discharge planning.

**Managing as Best I Can**

I pressed forward in spite of the situation. Big Boy was my motivation. I redirected my thoughts and focused on regaining my wellness in order to return home. I worked on upholding my enthusiasm and practicing a variety of coping strategies, which I had learned over the years.

I asked for a journal. I began to record my thoughts and experiences. When I was not writing, I was talking, walking, playing spades, or reading the Bible. Other times I prayed and would sing songs to myself and Big Boy in spirit. I spoke with him on the phone, but sometimes the conversations were cut short due to time constraints or when the phones were not available. My stepfather kept our family and my closest friends updated on my wellbeing. I was grateful for the support.

## Conclusion

The hospitalization was brief and lasted for seven days. This inpatient hospitalization was short compared to my experience in 2007, which lasted for three months. This was a blessing because my stay was long enough to concentrate on recovery priorities but short enough to reclaim my closeness with Big Boy.

When I returned home, I met with my treatment team—my psychiatrist and therapist. We created a plan of action. I had the same doctor for over eight years, and we decided to change my medication again. My therapist and I focused on enriching my self-care routine.

Over the next several weeks, I rebounded on better health by way of intense therapy. Our sessions focused on habits that promised positive results and balance. I was attentive to my sleeping habits, diet, meditations on the Bible, and enhanced routine. I got my life back! I hugged Big Boy more. I checked in with my circle of support and restored control of my livelihood.

Staying engaged in focused behaviors for individual wellbeing required practice. My support system actively helped me regroup. My treatment team played a significant role in helping me recuperate from the crisis. I changed my medication, wrote more often in my journal, updated my Wellness Recovery Action Plan, and developed a psychiatric advance directive.

Therefore, I encourage you to build trust in your treatment team and to create a solid network of support. I urge you to utilize practical coping tools to stay in your good place, working through challenges and pushing forward to your best life and your best self. I hope you will engage in the questions at the end of the chapters and share this book with others.

# 1

## STARTING THE CONVERSATION

There is a lot of stigma around mental illness. Yet, I share my recovery

story and people begin to open up.

---

**Blog Entry: January 6, 2015**

### Starting the Conversation

Limited information on mental illness leaves room for speculation and fear. This issue undoubtedly leads to worry and avoidance that fuels poor outlooks about mental health concerns. Therefore, mental illness needs to be discussed in order to reduce confusion, isolation, and propaganda. I share my story to promote the truth and to reduce stigma.

Generally, when I share my testimony, I get similar responses. People have said: "I know somebody with schizophrenia," or "I wish I would have talked to you sooner because your story helps me understand." This rekindles my desire to articulate my recovery story to offer hope. I share my experience to reduce the lies; *the lie* that recovery is not possible; *the lie* that life is over if you get a diagnosis, and another common misconception; *the lie* that we should not talk about it.

Sometimes people are reluctant to ask questions at the beginning of these group discussions, but I encourage the conversation. Mental health discussions offer insight and understanding that break down stigma. For me, sharing my story is therapeutic. I am in a safe place and talk about my condition in a constructive manner that offers awareness.

The misinformation circulated on schizophrenia - and related conditions - has an invisible muzzle that must be destroyed. My hope is that society will remove the mouthpiece and carry out more dialogue that reveals the truth. The truth is we can get better; we *can.* live fulfilling lives in recovery.

Finally, there needs to be a frank conversation on mental illness. These discussions will reduce stigma and help break the cycle of suffering. Talking about my mental illness helps strengthen my recovery and helps to combat stigma. Discussing my dark moments and joyous experiences with this diagnosis fights negative perceptions and provides insight that fosters understanding.

**Blog Entry: November 11, 2018**

## International Survivors of Suicide Day-

## November 17, 2018

According to the National institute of Mental Health, in 2016 "suicide was the second leading cause of death among individuals between the ages of 10 and 34, and the fourth leading cause of death among individuals between the ages of 35 and 54."

Everybody has a breaking point; perhaps an individual experiences a catastrophic event in life. Many individuals seek refuge but do not get what they need for recovery. Suicide is not a wish – it is a perceived source of relief when one feels they have limited options. Thoughts of taking one's own life are the by-product of a tormented mind. Common problems leading to suicide are financial issues, broken relationships, trauma, and untreated mental illness. Even though suicide is not limited to persons living with a mental illness, I will focus on the connection between these concerns.

Untreated mental illness could lead to premature death or suicide, despite age. There is a range of different signs and symptoms associated with mental illness. Experiencing these challenges - coupled with minimal coping strategies and limited access to resources - increases the risk of suicide.

Even though I have not attempted to take my own life, I realize that I was at risk. Before my diagnosis, I was not aware of my condition and did not engage in treatment. However, I know people who have attempted suicide. I learned from peers that repeated suicide attempts are common. As stated in the facts, children are not exempt from this issue. Suicide is more than a family issue; it is a societal problem.

WebMD identifies common signs that an individual may be suffering and at risk of suicide. Some of these indicators include:

- Withdrawal
- Changes in behavior
- Changes in appearance
- Making preparations

If you (or somebody you know), are at risk of suicide, I urge you to get help. There are crisis hotlines, Crisis Intervention Team (CIT) police officers, and mental health professionals who are qualified to help. The CIT officer is trained to deescalate situations and to take individuals who are in crisis to treatment facilities - not to jail. Professional support will be a strong asset to overcoming internal struggles and learning how to cope. I encourage us all to practice coping skills and to seek emergency resources for suicide and help.

November 17, 2018 is "International Survivors of Suicide Day." I anticipate that this day will be filled with recovery discussions to support suicide survivors, and to reduce the risk of suicide. I hope more people will research the facts about suicide and ensure access to professional care to reduce this issue. Here are some resources:

- National Suicide Prevention Hotline, call 1-800-273-8255, and
- Veteran Crisis Hotline, 1-800-273-8255.

**Blog Entry: December 8, 2018**

## Counseling Helps the Whole Person

When I started engaging in counseling 11 years ago, I assumed the scope of the sessions would focus on medicine and mental illness. However, nobody should assume. Counseling applies practical problem-solving to counteract the stresses of life. Counseling helps me manage concerns and develop recovery tools.

If you do not have experience with counselors, my experience will help you gain insight. There are several benefits to counseling; however, I will focus on three benefits to therapy. I will discuss the following key points:

1.  Counseling focuses on the whole person.
2.  Counseling encourages growth.
3.  Counseling can be ongoing.

First, a significant benefit of counseling is its focus on the whole person. The psychiatrist concentrates on treating symptoms and prescribing medication. However, counselors support doctor recommendations, and they are more attentive to our daily challenges. Therapy addresses more than medication – the sessions focus on managing life. Yes, we talk about side effects, the mental health condition, and how to manage recovery, but sessions also add balance to my life. Counseling helps me reflect on self-improvement.

Second, counseling encourages growth. The therapist is a great resource, and I appreciate my therapist for helping me identify strengths and opportunities to advance. I learned about the Certified Peer Specialist (CPS) training from my therapist. A Certified Peer Specialist (CPS) offers their experience, encouragement, and support to peers who are also in recovery.

The CPS position is a growing profession in the mental health field. The CPS training taught me how to articulate my recovery experience. The CPS training guided me on how I can motivate peers to overcome self-stigma, helping me mentor peers, and identifying strengths in order to focus on goals.

I enjoy motivating peers by sharing my recovery story and facilitating meetings. The Georgia Mental Health Consumer Network offers the CPS training and can be a great asset to states that do not offer this program yet. I became a CPS because my therapist identified an opportunity to enhance my skills as a mental health advocate.

Engaging in therapy does not have to be for a short period of time. I maintain counseling to work on myself and believe that ongoing counseling is the best answer for me. For example, therapy may be a great coping tool to help peers adjust to job changes, grief, relocation, relationships, and a broad range of transitions, which may be ongoing.

Counseling helps me maintain resiliency by pursuing self-improvement and acting on strengths. I encourage us all to view counseling as an option because counseling helps the whole person. Counseling is also available online (see Better Help on the Links and Resources page).

## End of Blog Entries

---

As a society, we must talk about mental illness to overcome stigma, suicide, and suffering. Untreated mental illness is a significant risk factor for suicide. Suicide is more than a family crisis; it is an epidemic. Even though I did not attempt suicide, I recognize that I was at risk, as my undiagnosed illness could have led to both aggressive thoughts and an eventual attempt on my own life. I have relatives and friends who are suicide survivors and realize that these issues do not go away on their own. Avoiding awareness – coupled with these challenges – only worsen the situation, preventing a healthy outlet and limiting access to professional treatment and care. Mental health challenges may not be preventable, but there is great potential to dramatically reduce suicide rates among us.

When I share my recovery story, it helps break down people's misconceptions and defenses, which leads to starting conversations on facts and getting help. Talking about mental health concerns with people who may not understand converts them into a supportive ally. Sharing my recovery story in safe places builds my self-confidence and breaks down the lingering aspects of the self-stigmatizing mindset.

Therapy focuses on a wide range of concerns and is beneficial to support the needs of the whole person. Therapy adds to the solution, helping combat a vast range of concerns. In my experience, therapy motivates me to enhance different aspects of my life. Counseling embodies a safe place to explore strengths and the need for improvement. My therapist challenges me and enables me to enrich my life. Lastly, these blog articles tap into the demand to start the conversation in order to bring down widespread negative perceptions, to save lives, and to empower people.

# My Self-Care Journal

1. Are you comfortable talking about mental illness? Would you feel more inclined to discuss mental health topics if society was more accepting of related concerns? _____

_____

_____

_____

_____

_____

_____

_____

_____

_____

_____

_____

_____

_____

_____

_____

_____

2. Is there a stigma around therapy? What are the benefits of participating in

therapy? _____

_____

_____

_____

_____

_____

_____

_____

_____

_____

_____

_____

_____

_____

_____

_____

_____

_____

_____

_____

_____

[This Page is Blank Intentionally for Notes]

[This Page is Blank Intentionally for Notes]

# 2

# DIS-SPELLING THE STIGMA

*I've been stigmatized on every side. Which is worst, the stigma that others place on us, or stigma internalized?*

---

**Blog Entry: November 21, 2018**

## Re-play on Janssen's Champions of Science: The Art of Ending Stigma- Panel Discussion

Shade. Labels. Darkness. Negativity. Secrets. Shame. Guilt. Hiding. Discrimination. These terms refer to the stigma of mental health conditions that worsen our experience, prolonging suffering and silence.

Janssen Pharmaceuticals' panel discussion about stigma is an important conversation. Dr. Adam Savitz (panelist, Janssen), Jeff Sparr (panelist, PeaceLove), myself (panelist), and Vickie Mabrey (moderator), held a lively hour-long discussion on Tuesday, November 13, 2018. We talked about a range of concerns that impact individuals in recovery. Jeff and I shared ways that we manage our condition and its challenges. Specifically, our coping skills embody artistic means of unique self-expression and creativity. Painting and writing play a significant role in our individual lifestyles.

A wide range of stigmatizing situations are common. We discussed how to manage concerns in the workplace through the department of Human Resources. Moreover, a psychiatric advance directive (PAD) is instrumental in maneuvering through a crisis. The plan is put in place when we are well, and the benefit of having a PAD is to help keep life moving smoothly despite the crisis.

A PAD is a document that controls how interventions are executed, giving us a voice in our lives during crisis, such as in our families, homes, pets, and bills, etc. The PAD is managed by individuals, chosen by us, and who we believe are best suited to help us through the situation. I learned that a PAD is a great coping tool in terms of resiliency. Having a PAD would have made managing my crisis easier and learning about PADs is just as important as insurance.

Janssen's panel discussion with Dr. Adam Savitz, Jeff Sparr, myself, and Vickie was an amazing experience. Watching this panel discussion will enrich your familiarity with on recovery. I encourage peers to get involved in recovery with self-expression, practical coping skills, and creativity. This will undoubtedly support our lives and help us manage.

Review Janssen Pharmaceuticals' *Champions of Science: The Art of Ending Stigma* website, and our panel discussion. The panel discussion offers empowering tips to live well (see Links and Resources page for information on the *Champions of Science: The Art of Ending Stigma* website).

**Blog Entry: March 8, 2019**

# The Role of the Therapist

The therapist upholds a firm foundation for my lifestyle. Therapy helps in diverse ways, helping me analyze various concerns that require attention. I maintain a better self-care routine when I engage in counseling.

Whenever I have unanswered questions with my doctor, I take these matters to my therapist, who helps me find answers. For example, when I had issues paying for medication, my therapist made a referral to manage my needs. In an emergency, my therapist assisted in scheduling appointments with my psychiatrist.

Overall, my therapist plays a vital role in helping me stay accountable to treatment, minimize self-stigma, and to stay focused on a holistic outlook. Holding onto negativity is easy. Therefore, being conscious of self-stigma is essential in managing recovery.

Limiting myself to the stereotypes that society places on us can weigh me down. Instead, I focus on my strengths that are referenced in therapy. I stay above self-stigma by reflecting on accomplishments, relationships, and my faith in God. I appreciate my therapists because they are resourceful, provide great input, and support my goals.

My therapist gives me assignments such as my mood journal; part of my accountability includes managing this journal, rating my moods on a daily basis according to a color-based scale. This journal helps depict the causes and effects of my mood that impact daily events.

My better days are the result of accomplishing my "things to do" list, while not-so-good days are typically plagued with unpredictable stress. My therapist and I review my mood journal and the corresponding events to identify my warning signs and triggers.

My holistic recipe includes spirituality and support. I aim to give God His time while I worship by praying, reading scriptures, and listening to uplifting music that focuses on Him. I feel at peace when I worship and meditate. Therapy not only helps me manage my mood but reinforces my commitments to enjoy recovery and life.

**Blog Entry: June 2, 2019**

# Help without Hope

Doctors have the gift of healing. They may perform miracles and restore wellness. If an individual needed surgery and had access to a surgeon, this would treat the person, restoring good health. This would be a great act of God. However, when the surgeon does *not* believe in the fruit of their works, this poses a threat. Why would a skilled surgeon perform the tasks and responsibilities of medicine if they did not believe in their craft? Likewise, why would mental health professionals limit our recovery?

A lot of us recall poor experiences with healthcare professionals. Unfortunately, these experiences are common. The mental health professional may state that a patient can never do what they used to do. Some healthcare professionals do not offer any hope, but only reinforce stigma and doubt. Other professionals do not say anything at all, leaving us without awareness, direction, or a sense of hope. *A poor prognosis can kill the spirit of recovery.*

I aim to reassure you that recovery is possible. We can overcome self-stigma and persevere through the highs and lows of our symptoms. Therefore, when a healthcare professional - or anybody - tells you what you cannot do, remind them that recovery is unique to each person. Trying to stay well is important; low expectations expressed by medical professionals and loved ones is hurtful. Therefore, cherish the healthcare professionals who are enthusiastic about recovery and offers guidance on how to manage better.

**Blog Entry: September 5, 2019**

## My Anti-Stigma Message: There is Hope

When I was diagnosed, there were not a lot of recovery stories on schizophrenia. The only story I could identify with was the movie, *Out of the Darkness*, featuring Diana Ross.

On a few occasions over the years, I have been called demonic due to my diagnosis. This is scary to me because I do not see myself as an evil spirit.

Others - ignorant of this condition and believing the many schizophrenia myths — may have thought I had been possessed by an evil spirit.

I was diagnosed at age 20. Now, I am a mental health advocate who aims to debunk myths, and I continue to strive to live well in recovery, despite the widespread stigma surrounding my disease.

I am appreciative of Janssen Pharmaceuticals' educational non-branded platform that aims to reduce stigma. In 2011, they spearheaded a documentary showing how recovery is possible for persons living with schizophrenia. This was the first time, I was seeing recovery in a positive light, as opposed to simply accepting that we were limited to the largely characterized symptom of hallucinations and voices. The half-hour film is titled: Living with Schizophrenia, A Call for Hope and Recovery (2011). This documentary features three recovery stories, including my own story, Josh Bell's, and Rebecca Phillips'.

In 2018, Janssen Pharmaceuticals led a panel discussion, which was an anti-stigma campaign. This virtual panel discussion featured: Vickie Mabrey (former ABC News Nightline Correspondent), Jeff Sparr (PeaceLove), Dr. Adam Savitz (Janssen), and myself. It is called Champions of Science: The Art of Ending Stigma.

Through this blog, I aim to offer hope and awareness. Moreover, I want to be an inspiring peer. So many of us are suffering in silence and do not have hope due to the stigma that society and others project onto us. This is the driving force behind my deep desire to share my story.

## End of Blog Entries

Discrimination and fear overlook individuality and minimizes recovery. However, policies create advantages. For example, health issues in the workplace may be addressed through the Human Resources department. A Psychiatric Advance Directive (PAD) acts as another insurance policy, providing preferences and guidance on how to help us when we need more support.

Moreover, therapy sheds light on inner strength in terms of overcoming self-stigmatizing perspectives, as well as managing the health issue and related concerns - such as its stigma. Sometimes a poor prognosis is given. However, there is hope because everybody is different and has varying strengths. Hope is essential to recovery because it helps dispel the pain and despair caused by discrimination, fear, shame, labels, and other stigmas that society holds against us. Some mental health professionals may perpetuate the stigma of mental illness, but not all. The therapist can help because they are resourceful, empathetic, and focused on finding answers and our strengths to press forward.

Famous stories of recovery about schizophrenia are limited. This is why I appreciate Janssen's non-branded awareness projects, such as the documentary, Living with Schizophrenia: A Call for Hope and Recovery, and the Champions of Science: The Art of Ending Stigma panel discussion. Furthermore, the stigma around schizophrenia fuels my passion to share my personal experience through the *Overcoming Schizophrenia* blog, offering hope and awareness.

# My Self-Care Journal

1. Identify ideal characteristics of a strong support system. If you do not have a strong support system, list potential associations, people and places where you could build stronger connections. _____

_____

_____

_____

_____

_____

_____

_____

_____

_____

_____

_____

_____

_____

_____

_____

_____

2. Reflect on a time when somebody told you that you could not achieve your goal, but you pressed forward anyway, accomplishing your objectives. What inspired you to keep moving forward? _____

_____

_____

_____

_____

_____

_____

_____

_____

_____

_____

_____

_____

_____

_____

_____

_____

_____

[This Page is Blank Intentionally for Notes]

Ashley Smith

[This Page is Blank Intentionally for Notes]

# 3

# PLANNING AHEAD

Hospitalization may play a role in living with this condition, however,

resiliency is a part of recovery.

**Blog Entry: November 30, 2018**

## Psychiatric Advance Directive (PAD): Discuss With Your Therapist and Loved Ones

Living with a mental illness is challenging, but organized interventions can help during a crisis. Planning ahead will maintain our decision-making preferences and independence. I was 20 years old when I was first hospitalized; I did not have a lot at risk. Unlike my first hospitalization, there was much at risk during my second hospitalization: my family. The information in this article will support newly diagnosed peers and those who have been in recovery for years. A crisis plan will help maneuver life during the stages of recuperation.

I learned an even greater lesson than "take your medication." The lesson I learned is not an innovative idea but sadly, an often overlooked one. I learned how a crisis plan could have alleviated a lot of my stress. The psychiatric advance directive (PAD) identifies decision-making preferences, delegated agents, and interventions. The National Alliance on Mental Illness (NAMI) defines the purpose of a psychiatric advance directive:

"A PAD allows a person to be prepared if a mental health crisis prevents them from being able to make decisions. A PAD describes treatment preferences, or names a person to make treatment decisions, should the person with a mental health condition be unable to make decisions."

NAMI's Peer-to-Peer Education Course identifies the psychiatric advance directive. A psychiatric advance directive is an empowering tool including, but not limited to, the following elements of documentation:

- Delegation of a primary decision-maker whenever an unspecified demand requires a decision to be made on behalf of the peer.
- A list of preferred facilities, treatment centers, and alternatives. Example: hospitals, respite centers, etc.
- A list of preferred medications.
- A list of medications to be avoided and reasons to justify

avoidance.

- Signs, or symptoms, which help the people who intervene determine when to activate the peer's PAD.

- Signs, and indications when the peer is in a better place to regain independent decision-making, and thus, minimize the guidance, and direction from the delegated agent in PAD.

- A list of supporters and their delegated responsibilities. Example: persons who will contact the peer's employer, landlord, review and pay bills, watch their home, and check the mail.

- Contact information specifying the treatment team, delegated agent, and other supporters.

- Signature page

When established this coping tool offers clarity on interventions. The PAD alleviates concerns. After hospitalization, we can focus on recuperating as opposed to being over-stressed with losses and problems. Examples of issues may be past due bills, poor communication with employers, an interruption in academic coursework, and altered living arrangements for our children and households. The PAD will undoubtedly enable us to bounce back from life's disruptions smoothly.

This document should be discussed with your therapist, who will guide you on how to get support for this plan of action, and how to implement the plan.

While it may be challenging to find a therapist, you may also seek online therapy (see Better Help in the Links and Resources page). Whether personally or online, speak with the therapist and the individuals who you want to be involved in your PAD; this will enforce its effectiveness.

**Blog Entry: March 7, 2019**

## Peer-to-Peer Advice

When I was diagnosed with schizophrenia 12 years ago, my doctor gave me two pieces of information: (1) take your medication, and (2) manage your stress. Since then, I managed my household, part-time job, and family - underestimated the importance of stress management. I was hospitalized last year due to what seemed like a decade of stress.

In short, warning signs and triggers are awareness indicators, helping us to identify threats to wellness. These signs are similar yet different, like a stop sign versus a yield sign on the road. Warning signs alert an individual that they are not feeling well and require attention to manage both symptoms and the situation. They may be subtle or major: changes in appetite, sleeping habits, and routine may be warning signs.

Triggers are experiences that create negative consequences, either emotionally, physically, socially, or legally. A trigger might be going to a place that reminds an individual of a poor experience. Accordingly, this trigger creates tension and dread that leads to irritability, poor communication, and eventually, chaos. The advice my doctor gave worked well, and I learned how recovery is more manageable when I am aware of my warning signs and triggers.

Finally, I encourage us all to create an individualized recovery plan. If the medication works well, continue treatment; however, also use additional coping tools, such as a crisis plan. An excellent guide for recovery is Mary Ellen Copeland's WRAP [Wellness Recovery Action Plan], or a psychiatric advance directive (PAD). They provide instructions on how to facilitate interventions in spite of the crisis.

These Plans share pertinent information, such as how a peer functions when she or he is well, and when more support is required. These plans identify preferences, warning signs, and triggers that effectively offer support when our health demands it. A plan is essential because it acknowledges many factors to help enrich lives despite medical setbacks. As one peer to another, I encourage us to develop a recovery intervention such as the WRAP or PAD, helping us to maintain wellness and regain control of our lives after a crisis.

**Blog Entry: August 20, 2019**

## Parenting With Mental Illness and Crisis

I am a lived experience expert on schizophrenia, having persevered through a range of issues related to my diagnosis. I have been in recovery for a few years and experienced a lot related to the symptoms of my condition, court-ordered hospitalizations, housing discrimination, and projected stereotypes. Common misconceptions create stereotypes, which in turn places us in a box, not of our own making. Still, I work on myself and press forward. In this article, I share my experience as a peer in recovery, but also how I managed as a *parent in crisis*. I am a mother of a seven-year-old child.

I engage in therapy and traditional treatment to help maintain wellness. I practice a lot of coping skills to manage every day - I take walks, journal, and listen to music, and other self-care activities. I rely on my support network, treatment team, and daily coping tools to get through challenges and crises.

Last year I endured a crisis that created significant challenges. Fortunately, my family and friends helped me manage, assisting with parenting responsibilities and communicating needs with specific individuals who needed to know. We maneuvered the hospital setting and my household affairs. I am grateful for my support system because with their assistance, I was able to focus on recuperating and meeting the demands placed on myself, as well as the needs of my son.

When I returned home, I focused on regrouping. I participated in intense therapy sessions over a few weeks with an emphasis on stress management and a self-care routine. I demonstrated a speedy recovery through the aid of my supporters and the determination to activate all the coping skills I learned. As a result of enduring the process of hospitalization, crisis, and recuperation, I was able to manage better and avoid another crisis.

Earlier this year, I took a small break to minimize stress and to avoid a crisis. I felt overwhelmed. I communicated my needs with family, and we developed a plan to have Big Boy cared for as I regrouped, staying in a respite center for a few days. In Georgia, we have peer-led respite centers located throughout the state; these are community-oriented places to interact with peers and focus on wellness. I engaged in group activities and got a lot of rest.

My support system and I managed the crisis and prevented a significant setback. With my network of support, I was able to regroup, maintain my mommy role, and utilize the respite center to concentrate on maintaining wellness. These experiences reinforced the importance of a support system. We executed plans that enabled me to get my needs met for better health, while also addressing necessary care for my child.

## End of Blog Entries

---

Crisis may occur, and how we cope is a vital concern. Having a crisis plan minimizes stress and protects our livelihood. Throughout the chapter, "Planning Ahead," I share many factors that contribute to the development of a crisis plan which allows us to focus on recuperation.

When I was hospitalized, I did not have my Wellness Recovery Action Plan (WRAP) with me, nor did I have a psychiatric advance directive (PAD). Reflecting on the aftermath of my hospitalization, I now recognize the many benefits of having these plans on file. Understanding that these documents are vital to maneuvering thought life's highs and lows will encourage you to create and keep a current plan in place. Like insurance policies, they do not prevent crisis, however, *they reduce the ramifications of them.* Use WRAPs and PADs to help minimize stress and master resiliency!

Our support system is an essential force in implementing this plan of action. Throughout the process, I emphasize our role as the captain of the team, playing a major role in my own success. Mary Ellen Copeland's Wellness Recovery Action Plan (WRAP) workbook covers the foundation of recovery and includes a collection of wellness tools. The WRAP workbook guides us through the development of essential coping mechanisms, outlining the blueprint of the psychiatric advance directive (PAD). (See Links and Resources on Wellness Recovery Action Plan (WRAP), and the National Resource Center on Psychiatric Advance Directives, for detailed information on obtaining resources).

Finally, respite centers are places to regroup. They are not hospitals or medical facilities, but instead, they serve as hubs for peers to focus on self-development in recovery. Mental illness may be a part of our lives, but we can be strong, finding balance and triumph - no matter what.

# My Self-Care Journal

1. Identify coping skills that others use to manage life. How might you include these coping skills to better manage? _____

_____

_____

_____

_____

_____

_____

_____

_____

_____

_____

_____

_____

_____

_____

_____

_____

2. What is most valuable to you? How can the WRAP or PAD protect your

livelihood? _____

_____

_____

_____

_____

_____

_____

_____

_____

_____

_____

_____

_____

_____

_____

_____

_____

_____

_____

_____

[This Page is Blank Intentionally for Notes]

[This Page is Blank Intentionally for Notes]

# 4

# COPING TAKES WORK

I realized my mental health condition requires more than a routine. It demands work to master coping tools that support my wellness.

---

**Blog Entry: November 9, 2014**

## My Medication Schedule

Recently, I changed my medication schedule. For the last two months, I had problems staying asleep, so I spoke with my psychiatrist to resolve these concerns. We discovered I was taking one of my prescriptions at night when I should have taken it in the morning; I had altered my medication regimen for convenience. I will return to the morning routine, and I will set my cell phone alarm as a reminder to take my medication.

I am hopeful this change will help me sleep better. It is interesting how small adjustments can create big problems – or solutions. I expect my sleep patterns to improve, along with my energy level at work. How do you manage your routine and medication regimen?

**Blog Entry: January 22, 2019**

## Therapy Builds Self-Awareness and Relationships

When I was diagnosed with mental illness over 11 years ago, I did not know what to expect. Various relationships helped me maneuver life's challenges, and my partner played an essential role in my support system. Strengthening communication and addressing needs with him is crucial to managing my life.

Still, an individual must understand and know themselves. I am a partner, advocate, and spiritual individual. My experience has shown me how a lack of familiarity with my condition and coping skills can lead to unnecessary problems in my relationship.

The symptoms of my condition may manifest as irritability, moodiness, and anxiety - among many other indicators. Therapy helps me become more mindful of my condition and its symptoms, enabling me to manage my relationship with my partner. I will share three tips for getting the most from counseling; these help me prosper in self-awareness and in my intimate relationship.

In the past, I hesitated and struggled with accepting new medications, fearing the effects they might have on me. I delayed trying the new anti-depressants, but my therapist helped me anticipate the common potential side effects. After moving forward with the new medication, proper adjustments were made to prevent any unwelcome reactions.

Writing is a significant coping skill for me, helping me articulate ideas, record events, and offer self-awareness. Once, a therapist suggested I share my journal entries in our session to provide extra insight; this was a a great strategy because it helped me express the concerns I was having. Eventually, my therapist recommended I start a "mood journal."

Reflecting on my mood journal provided insights as to my mood swings and their impact on my relationships. These insights proved helpful to my therapist and I in pinpointing warning signs and triggers, as well as in developing ways to manage my condition and my relationships.

In the doctor's office, we may be asked about our level of pain based on a scale of 1 to 10, one meaning no pain, and ten indicating a lot of pain. Instead of using a numeric scale, I chose a color-coded scale for my mood journal, creating it on the basis of the color-coded behavior system used in my son's elementary school. My color-coded system uses the following colors: pink, purple, blue, green, yellow, orange, and red. "Pink" signifies an excellent day, "purple" a great day, "blue" a good day, and "green" is ready for the day. The colors; yellow, orange, and red illustrate escalating poor moods.

Likewise, my mood journal is a great method into identifying patterns, enhancing my relationships by being mindful of those swings in emotional states, then finding ways to reduce the triggers causing them. My experience with therapy helps me develop self-awareness for the betterment of all my relationships, but especially with my partner. Whenever I work on myself through counseling, I see positive results, adding balance to my life. Therefore, I encourage us all to engage in therapy for wellness and healthier relationships with ourselves and our partners.

## End of Blog Entries

---

In summary, everyday habits (such as keeping a daily mood journal and maintaining my medication schedule), as well as my commitment to counseling, have been essential in my recovery. If we are to strengthen our intimate relationships, we must do the work of identifying warning signs and triggers that threaten those relationships, as well as engaging in therapy to find solutions for our challenges.

# My Self-Care Journal

1. Have your symptoms created challenges for any of your relationships? How might a mood journal support your recovery? _____

_____

_____

_____

_____

_____

_____

_____

_____

_____

_____

_____

_____

_____

_____

_____

_____

_____

2. What does your routine look like? Identify two self-care habits that work

well for you_____

_____

_____

_____

_____

_____

_____

_____

_____

_____

_____

_____

_____

_____

_____

_____

_____

_____

_____

Ashley Smith

[This Page is Blank Intentionally for Notes]

[This Page is Blank Intentionally for Notes]

# 5

# I CHOOSE TO LIVE

There are many obstacles I can dwell on. However, I believe I will overcome no matter what distractions pop up, therefore, I am focusing on what I did well.

---

**Blog Entry: October 20, 2018**

## Coping In The Spirit

I am fighting my schizoaffective disorder every day through spirituality. A combination of mania, the side effects of medication, and concerns with self-motivation are frequent challenges for me. Still, I aim to stay well-balanced by practicing a variety of coping skills which include communicating my needs with my treatment team and sharing concerns with those individuals within my circle. I reflect on my relationships, self-care, and responsibilities on a constant basis. Currently, I am challenged by controlling my high energy. I maintain hope.

I manage my schizophrenia and bipolar disorder through faith in God. I cling to my faith when taking my medication and focus on staying optimistic and practicing self-care rituals for maintenance. Every day, I strive to push forward and hold on to hope by concentrating on self-care and stress management activities. I incorporate relaxation into my daily routine by engaging in a lot of activities such as taking walks, completing word search puzzles, doing house chores, reading inspirational material, listening to music, and writing in my journal.

While my mental illness can create a lot of stress and problems, I choose to live well through faith and hope, reading scriptures and meditating on the Bible to overcome any negative energy and anxiety. The following scriptures inspire me: Isaiah 38:15-17, Ecclesiastes 7:13, and Psalm 139:13-18.

These scriptures give me hope, keeping me close to The One. Despite being in recovery for many years I am still open to information, ways to cope, and changes to my self-care plan. I share my lived experience with my minister, hoping it might empower others, as well.

When I journal, I record daily reflections about God; these may include scriptures, prayers, and affirmations. My *Overcoming Schizophrenia* blog is my journal for– and to God. Also, I created a special prayer and affirmation for you:

*My God, my God. Thank You. I thank You for another opportunity to share my story, reaching someone who needs validation and reassurance. You love me the way I am, and I am grateful. I know I am loved even when – during trials and mind wars - I do not show love to myself as strongly as You do. I give thanks for my life. I love You and need You. I will overcome with Your help – and on your schedule – because it is already done. Amen.*

Lastly, I leave you with this scripture that inspires me to share my recovery journey and to continue coping in the Spirit: Proverbs 31:8 New Living Translation (NLT): "Speak up for those who cannot speak for themselves…" Thank you, take care.

**Blog Entry: January 29, 2019**

# The Therapist Helps: Accept Your Assignment for Your Relationship

Stress management plays a significant role in my mental health challenges. As I grow in my recovery, I learn how to distinguish moods, symptoms, and my characteristics that sometime impact my relationship with myself and my partner. Most days are good. That said, my mood fluctuates based on expectations and daily events.

Relationships create stress, but this is a part of life. Good stress (the effort it takes to improve my life) and not-so-good stress impact my mental health. Counseling provides a great help in coping with - and tolerating - my condition and disappointments. Whenever I feel overtaxed, my mood becomes irritable and my memory is not as sharp. One sign of stress is being in a negative place and wanting to isolate.

I am grateful for access to therapy because of the positive effects on my relationships. Insight from a professional adds balance to my perspective which, in turn, helps with stress management. As I discover more about myself, I understand how vital therapy can be in my life, and especially in my relationship with my significant other.

My therapist helps me process my better days and bad days. A good day to me is when I manage a rigorous routine yet maintain balance through relaxation. My relaxation looks like listening to different types of music, dancing to upbeat music, and spending time with family and friends.

Bad days require more self-care in response to internal and external stresses. For me, these days look like lack of motivation to perform simple tasks, dwelling on problems, and the loss of a productive self-care routine.

Engaging in counseling helps me identify areas I need to work on, and one of the greatest benefits involves accepting challenging assignments that build self-awareness. The mood journal (and accompanying color-code scale) is a useful and necessary tool for tracking my state of mind, as well as reflecting warning signs and crisis-triggers. I enjoy reviewing my journal, as it reminds me how I can have a direct effect on managing myself and surviving difficult times.

When I engage in repetitive self-care rituals, my stress levels are reduced. I create affirmations, walk to clear my mind, and listen to motivational talks that inspire me. My therapist recommends that I keep a "realistic agenda," I keep a "realistic agenda," which my therapist also recommended. Opposed to a list of things to do, I uphold a realistic agenda that is a list of accomplished tasks. This agenda inspires me to seek results opposed to adding pressure based on the tasks that I did not complete.

To manage all of my needs, I focus on my whole person. The assignments offered in counseling provide another perspective on how to enhance self-care and getting effective results. My therapist helps me talk with my doctor by – for example - role playing, articulating side effects and problems that my doctor and I can then work through. Therapy is a great coping tool, for me because it creates empowering assignments that stimulate personal growth, while readying me for doctor visits.

**Blog Entry: April 30, 2019**

## Break through the Illness Web: Redefine Recovery

Living with mental illness is not an option. Recovery is. What is recovery? In the beginning, I did not understand my diagnosis nor how recovery works, so I borrowed my vision of recovery from others. My enthusiastic state hospital doctor said I could return to school, which I did. My mother told me she could see me sharing with others about how I coped with schizophrenia. In 2008, I started this blog.

Another pivotal influence shaping my outlook on living with schizophrenia was seeing another individual with my diagnosis facilitate a course. WRAP, classes guide us on how to develop an individualized recovery plan to overcome relapse. Participating in these classes inspired me to become a Certified Peer Specialist (CPS).

A CPS is a someone with a mental health challenge who supports peers in recovery by sharing personal stories of resiliency. Breaking through the illness web involves overcoming poor societal views, redefining recovery, and creating a new perception of self.

After 12 years of recovery I realize that my definition of recovery involves striving to maintain my "good place," breaking through the illness web by way of changing my perspectives on recovery, and dis-spelling self-stigma by living my best life. This definition of recovery has evolved over the years. In the past, I defined recovery in different ways that included:

1) to restore

2) to maintain medication compliance, and

3) to stay out of the hospital

These definitions of recovery covered different phases of my life. A peer shared a different perspective on the meaning of recovery, defining it as self-improvement. He does not want to restore his old self; instead he focuses on the future and improving who he is.

While I take medication to manage my symptoms, it is not effective single-handedly. I was on medication despite my breakdown last year [2018].

Recovery cannot be based on staying out of the hospital because I am dealing with a brain disorder. Last year's hospitalization ignited another phase in my recovery – growth. Remember: my definition of recovery is to keep trying to stay in a good place; while that definition of recovery may change for me, for the moment, it helps me to break through the illness web.

## End of Blog Entries

---

The title of this chapter, "I Choose to Live," focuses on my understanding of how to manage coping tools. I focus on thriving in my recovery lifestyle through unique self-care agendas, my therapy, coping skills, mood journal, realistic journal, and definition of recovery.

Moreover, my faith and outlook on recovery enables me to conquer self-stigma by focusing on self-improvement. Therapy is helpful in meeting my recovery needs, and I encourage us all to try therapy to balance wellness and relationships. Although I have a mental illness, I am in love with the process - and with my journey.

I am enough - in terms of my efforts at managing my condition - because I have the coping tools to master resiliency and faith in the process of my recovery. Hope is the foundation of my recovery. It has become clearer over the years; I am overcoming self-stigma and the issues associated with schizophrenia *because I have hope for my future.*

# My Self-Care Journal

1. How firm is your recovery foundation? _____

_____

_____

_____

_____

_____

_____

_____

_____

_____

_____

_____

_____

_____

_____

_____

_____

_____

2. Articulate two areas of your life that you feel you need to consider working on with a therapist. _____

_____

_____

_____

_____

_____

_____

_____

_____

_____

_____

_____

_____

_____

_____

_____

_____

_____

_____

_____

_____

[This Page is Blank Intentionally for Notes]

[This Page is Blank Intentionally for Notes]

# 6

# FINAL WORDS

My mother told me I would share with others about how I made it through
with schizophrenia, and I believed her…

---

Living with a brain disorder can be difficult for several reasons. We have an
invisible illness that many people do not understand; many fear it,
projecting their negative stereotypes onto us. Sadly, we often succumb,
feeding into discouragement, but we do not have to stay in that negative
place. The most disturbing that effects stigma can inflict on us is when we
internalize these negative beliefs and stop striving to live our best lives.
Stigma may be an issue for others, but self-stigma does not have to be one
*for us.*

We all have a story. Schizophrenia and related conditions are a part of ours,
but it does not have to be the end of our story. We all have limitations, but
we also have strengths. We can choose to transform this medical challenge
into a strength by modeling our own values in recovery. That is the act of
applying unique coping strategies to create a hopeful and well life while

maintaining individuality and diverse recovery lifestyles to defeat self-stigma.

Life will create turbulent situations that we must aim to overcome. The world may view living with mental health conditions as a setback, threat, or a foreign medical condition. While living with these conditions may feel like we are holding the weight of the world, we must keep fighting for our lives. Fortunately, we can choose to concentrate on our strengths and to overcome the impact of widespread negative perspectives.

## Another Look at the Lessons Learned

There is no such thing as *mind over matter* when dealing with psychosis and delusions. I could not control the racing thoughts, bizarre beliefs, nor tame my elevated energy and the multitude of symptoms prior to my crisis. However, I could have acted on my warning signs and triggers by alerting my network of support and working on a wide range of my coping techniques to help persevere prior to the onset of my triggers.

The Wellness Recovery Action Plan or psychiatric advance directive are effective interventions when organized and put into motion during a place of wellness. Having discussions with our caregiver and closest supporters will deliver better outcomes for recuperation. (See Links and Resources for direction to these guides on personal development).

Again, medication cannot treat all symptoms nor tame crisis, but evidence of recovery prevails. Yes, hospitalization may play a role in living with schizophrenia and related conditions. Yet, resiliency is also a part of recovery. It takes hard work to try over and over again, but we can.

My experience demonstrates how hospitalizations may be inevitable in spite of efforts to maintain wellness. Adherence to medication compliance did not prevent last year's hospitalization. Lack of attention to my warning signs coupled with the steadily growing severe symptoms of my illness led to major confusion and ultimately crisis. I hope this book will motivate you to try therapy and to never give up on striving to stay in a place of self-awareness, with dedication to practicing coping skills and maintaining self-care.

At its worst, living with my severe and persistent mental illness - while experiencing its dreadful symptoms -was ruthless. Still, I found the motivation to persist in terms of regaining my peace and winning the battle for recovery. *Resiliency is utilizing effective tools to press forward in response to setbacks.* Hospitalization may be a part of living with this condition, but mastering resiliency by the art of performing multiple unique coping mechanisms is the driving force that defines my recovery.

## Practical Coping Skills

It is important to understand our individual stressors and coping tools. I hope that you take heed of warning signals and understand your triggers. Engaging in recovery by involving yourself in therapy and crisis planning can undermine the myth that recovery is not possible. I urge you to take ownership of recovery by practicing unique coping skill and using your therapist as an ally in your recovery lifestyle.

However, do not simply sign up for therapy and then fail to participate in the wellness exercises and process of growth. Guide your therapist about areas in which you seek insight to effectively manage and to cope with life's challenges. If therapy did not work in the past, try again.

## Recovery Principles

Living with schizophrenia and related conditions can make life more complicated but using practical coping skills will help. We may all face dreadful situations that lead to crisis. Practice your coping tools and never give up hope, because recovery is possible. Concentrate on investing in a health plan that specifically supports your needs; mental illness is a life-long medical condition that requires ongoing management.

Holding on to a vision of hope is powerful. Finding motivation to try again and trusting the process to reclaim our lives *is priceless*. I encourage you to continue to press forward through the highs and lows on this recovery journey. If you do not have a vision for your recovery, borrow mine. Strive for a better place with your support system, using different wellness tools. Stay focused on your motivation to make resiliency efforts a part of your life, because you are worth it.

Let your recovery trump myths, giving you the full life that you deserve. Recovery is about the spirit of resiliency, the act of getting up when you are knocked down - and trying again. Lastly, crisis and self-stigma are hard to endure, but "it's not the load that breaks you down, it's the way you carry it," –Lena Horne

# AFTERWORD

## Three Pieces of Wisdom to Ensure A Safe Place

Formerly published in CURESZ Foundation Newsletter, April 2019

I was 20 years old when I experienced my first hospitalization. When I was first diagnosed my doctor gave me two pieces of advice, (1) take your medicine, and (2) manage your stress. My second and last hospitalization occurred at the age of 31. I gained a lot of wisdom in this 11-year gap between hospitalizations. One important parcel of wisdom was how to – and why t0 - create a post-crisis plan. I encourage peers in recovery to make plans for the future.

As I recovered between the two hospitalizations, I became better equipped with coping skills. I re-created my personalized Wellness Recovery Action Plan (WRAP) and I found I was finally able to manage well by engaging in focused behaviors for my wellbeing.

At the age of twenty, I did not understand my diagnosis of schizophrenia - or that recovery was possible. In fact, my undiagnosed symptoms led me to encounter both my first hospitalization *and legal issues*. I was anxious, afraid, and experienced a wide range of symptoms including hallucinations, psychosis, delusions and paranoia. My hallucinations frightened me. I did not know what hallucinations were, and thus, could not articulate the symptoms. My hallucinations included exaggerated evil cartoon-like voices telling me I was a dishonor to my family.

In addition to those cartoon-like voices, multiple other voices clouded my thinking, disrupting my ability to engage in conversations. While different hallucinations continued to scare me, I believed the same person was stalking me; I could not outrun or escape him/her. I was certain that strangers knew me, watched me, and talked about me. Moreover, these hallucinations scared me so badly I ended up stealing a military pick-up truck, went on a high-speed chase to escape the police, the demons, my many mind wars, and haunting thoughts. My living nightmare got worse when I was jailed and hospitalized for five months.

Fortunately, my diagnosis set me free with this newly found knowledge, experience, and treatment, saving my life from the ongoing nightmare which was my undiagnosed schizophrenia. Between age 20 and 31, I participated in a clubhouse for young adults (ages 16-24) with mental illness. I stayed for almost a year, entrenched in the program which provided therapy, housing, a safe haven for us to relate and socialize without stigma, and recovery-oriented classes such as Mary Ellen Copeland's WRAP, and learning how to apply for disability income Afterwards, I became involved with NAMI Georgia, otherwise known as the National Alliance on Mental Illness. Through the years, I created a strong support system including peers, family, and my treatment team. I engaged online, and created a blog, Overcoming Schizophrenia.

In 2018, my second hospitalization proved these supports worked well for my recovery. My diagnosis is now schizoaffective disorder. My significant stress load - not poor medication compliance - led to my last hospitalization. Fortunately, with the aid of my support system, learned coping skills, and my hope of reuniting with my son, I was in and out of the hospital and in a safe, fulfilling, and positive place faster.

I would like to see peers reach that same safe place faster, as I did. Taking medication, working on stress management, and developing a post-crisis plan have been vital to my recovery.

# APPENDIX A

## Beautiful Scars

### By Brian Anderson, CPS/CRE

I am a Certified Peer Specialist and Certified Recovery Educator (CPS/CRE). I have a genuine compassion for those in need. Life has not always been easy for me. At the age of five, I was homeless with my father and two older brothers. We slept in a car without money and food. We did not know what would happen next. Periodically, a family would allow us to sleep on their floor for a couple of days. However, as time passed, we became homeless again. Around the age of 7 or 8, I was molested by one of the families that took us in. I kept this secret hidden from my family, and father, because I did not want us to be kicked out onto the streets, and back living in a car without warmth and food.

My learning suffered because I was taken away from my mother, molested, and homeless. I was ridiculed by students because I could not read or write well. In addition to this, I was known as the "smelly" little boy. As a result of being homeless, there was no money to buy soap, brush my teeth, or to wash my clothes. All these situations led to a spiraling road of mental illness, drug addiction, self-hatred, three times jailed, chronic homelessness as a young adult, two suicide attempts, lock down in-patient treatment, and more.

With the help of God, a praying father, and having gone through a lot, change eventually came. Now, I can proudly say I have been on various television networks such as TBN, Atlanta Live, and several local radio stations in Georgia. My books are endorsed by leading mental health professionals and are utilized as teaching tools. As an individual who has recovered from homelessness, hopelessness, drug addiction, molestation, mental illness, jail, suicidal ideation, and more, I have a strong devotion to help others on their road to recovery and healing.

I use a few tools and coping techniques on my journey through recovery. I have faith and total trust in the God of my understanding. When life gets dark for me, which it still does at times, I choose to "believe in the dark" that I am going to make it, because I know God will! My definition to know is to have an intimate relationship with God. I use "I Am" statements, such as "I am more than enough," "I am blessed," "I am favored," "I am beautiful," and more. I learned there is power in what I say, because words have power. I laugh with every chance that I get. Laughter is good for the soul. Even fake laughter makes me feel better. So, I choose laughter every day.

I must give back. This peer work is truly a part of who I am. I give what I need. Every day I must give hope, love, and peace. I believe that we reap what we sow, and we will receive what we give. Lastly, I choose to motivate everybody that I meet. I believe I must motivate with love and with every breath that I take. My motivation mixed with love will leave a ripple effect on this world, and the lives of others long after I am gone. One love.

# APPENDIX B

## The Point Will Stay True

by Terresa Ford, CPS, CPRP

I had a ray of light in my darkest days. Her name was Molly. She was my painting teacher for more than ten years. Molly had a saying, "If a brush is good, the point will stay true."

She was talking about quality paint brushes, however, I heard something different. What I understood was that if I stayed on course, I would prevail. Recovery for me is the reclamation of my authentic life on my own terms; the act of living a life of my choosing. Sounds simple, but extremely complicated when you add a severe and persistent mental illness like schizophrenia.

My coping strategies are intentional, holistic and based in my spiritual practices. I paint almost every day, even for just fifteen minutes. I pray every day several times a day for guidance, clarity and to maintain my "right" mind. Exercise and a healthy diet are also a big part of my life.

Medication and counseling help me manage my symptoms, but it is the act of working to know, love, and serve my Creator through Catholicism that grounds me.

In another life I was an arts administrator designing art education programs for art museums. For the past seven years I have been working as a Certified Peer Specialist in clinical settings. I am certified to facilitate Hearing Voices Network peer support groups. Since my diagnosis of schizophrenia in 2015, I have been driven to use my lived experience to empower others to live a life of their choosing.

Currently, I am working towards my second Master's degree at Emory University, Candler School of Theology. Through all my adversities, I can say the brush is good and the point has stayed true.

# APPENDIX C

## Breaking The Cycle

By Stacey Walker, Sr., CPS

I am a disabled combat veteran that has served three combat tours. Still, I am capable of defending the freedom and values of this great nation. My story did not begin with a mental health diagnosis. When I was younger, I had unwanted and distorted images that were explained away with dismissive clichés, which I felt was a camouflage for calling me crazy. I kept to myself and continued to have these frightening distorted images and voices.

Eventually, I convinced myself that the images were normal, and everyone was able to see and hear what I could. Some of you may identify with some of these experiences; various types of abuse, poverty, neglect, shame, fear, and embarrassment. These are a summary of terms that describe my childhood that broke me, and also shaped me. I became molded me into a passive person. I also became a very angry person, all the while very willing to please and eager to show my worth. This shell of anger protected me and allowed me to endure the abuse. After all, boys are not supposed to show emotion or vulnerability.

The desire to be noticed and loved, drove me to work harder than everyone else, but the desire to please led me to more abuse and sexual addiction in my early teen years. I eventually left home at age 17, because the abuse had become too much. The anger and rage started to manifest in dangerous ways. Finally, a period of homelessness put me in a severe state of depression. I was in complete survival mode.

One day on a six mile walk to work in the early morning darkness it dawned on me that I was not taking care of myself and was lost. Fortunately, I was able to get into a program where I received purpose direction and motivation. I also met my wife. Things were good for a while and I was even able to prosper a little. Most importantly during this time, I qualified to join the US Army.

Finally, I found where I fit. Where everything made sense. I thrived in this environment because I lived it all my life. Anger and aggression finally had a home and it was valuable in this profession. Then came the invasion of Iraq in 2003. I was on duty inside our operating base and a rocket propelled grenade came over the wall and exploded roughly 10 meters away. I was dazed and confused. The debris to my face cost me eight stiches over my right eye and I later learned it caused mild traumatic brain injury. I returned home, recovered from the impact of this explosion, returned to duty and almost immediately received orders to redeploy. One day on a reconnaissance mission in northern Iraq shots rang out. While scrambling for cover I tore my Achilles tendon. I had to be medically evacuated. Upon returning home I had my sixth war-related surgery and was not able to walk for most of 2012. I was devastated and enraged. I had fallen from elite status and felt cast aside.

During this time, wartime images replaced my childhood delusions and those familiar voices returned, only this time trying to comfort me, or so I thought. I became very aggressive to those whom I viewed as the enemy. I was in so much pain every day for years that I began mixing cocktails of pills just to report for duty. I was so fixated on the control that I had in war zones and often could not tell the difference between home and being in the desert. I would stay awake for days checking the doors at home and I was suspicious of everything. I realized that my relationship with my family was not the same for a while. I could not feel anything and even though I worked tirelessly helping my friends, it turns out they all feared who I had become.

Over the years I reached out to behavioral health providers several times for help and was told that I was experiencing these things from a lack of sleep, but the voices and the rage kept telling me that it was so much more. It seemed that if I performed my duties in exemplary fashion, nobody cared about my issues. It was always mission first. One day, after working more than 30 consecutive hours, I was provoked by my senior non-commissioned officer about a simple matter. To make a long story short, I was arrested for attempted felony assault on three of my command staff leaders. I was committed to Martin Army Community Hospital on Ft. Benning, Georgia for nearly two weeks, where for the first time in my life, I got the help I needed. I slept like never before and my mind finally turned off.

It was there where I began to understand that the unwanted, distorted images and voices of my childhood were not common. They were symptoms of mental illness. As a result, the charges were dropped and I received several diagnoses of severe depression, Post Traumatic Stress Disorder with psychotic features and obsessive-compulsive disorder. After leaving the hospital I continued to struggle with my anger. Fortunately, under the new medications, I was better able to manage my anger.

Soon after, I was notified that I would be discharged from the Army. I felt betrayed. I had devoted my life to the Army, but now that I had a mental health diagnosis, I was no longer essential. I fully identified with being a soldier and I could not suddenly turn that off. Even though I felt isolated, I was learning how to ask for help.

It was late 2014 when I found a balance of faith and medication that worked for me. I found purpose and healing by volunteering at a Christian Mission where I began to learn from my peers about recovery. For example, I learned that recovery is a lifestyle where it is my responsibility to pursue. I also found that advocating for my peers motivates me to maintain my own mental health and wellness.

Lastly, I learned how my relationships with family and peers are the cornerstone of my recovery. My life goals are to become a professional speaker to educate, motivate, and encourage recovery through faith and treatment. Based on my lived experience, I would like to share several suggestions. To my peers, I implore you to take advantage of any opportunity to make a difference by telling your stories. To the Behavioral Health System, I implore you to focus on an individual and holistic approach to each person. Thank you for reading my story.

# APPENDIX D

## The Heart of Recovery

By Pat Strode, Caregiver

As a family member of someone in recovery with mental illness, I have had to come to terms with the fact that recovery is not only a personal journey, it also has no time limit. Just as treatment for mental illness is individualized, so is the recovery journey. Coming to terms with this understanding also means that my relative's recovery is solely theirs; it was not, and is not about me, or what I think recovery should look like.

I have a role with providing support, being patient, educating myself about mental illness, and learning about systems of care to promote recovery. I advocate for improvements in different systems, but not solely for my loved one. I advocate for everybody who receives services. It is important to me to understand that a foundation in faith and hope are essential, especially when relapses occur in recovery. It is faith and hope that has fueled my advocacy for nearly 25 years and has become a vital part of my self-care.

# APPENDIX E

Subject: Letter to the Caregiver

Dear Caregiver,

The role of a caregiver is priceless to us. You carry a lot of responsibilities that help us cope with our mental health conditions. Your efforts to support our recovery go beyond the title of "caregiver." Your position in our lives demand strong bonds, which encompasses trust and respect for individuality.

Although my caregiver lives in another state, he upholds a vital role in my life that helps me maintain recovery. My stepfather, the man who raised me, is my caregiver. In 2018, I voluntarily went to the hospital. This act was a difficult - but necessary – decision. As evidence of my trust in my stepfather's advice, I accepted his request and admitted myself into the emergency room.

Shared decision-making plays a significant role in winning the battle against mental illness. My hope is that you uphold trust in order to maintain the shared decision-making relationship. As caregivers, you are our care-partner in this war against stigma and how mental illness impacts our lives. I encourage you to keep advocating for us, practicing shared decision-making, and - more importantly - valuing our trust. Thank you.


Warm Regards,

Ashley Smith

# APPENDIX F

Subject: Letter to the Therapist

Dear Therapist,

One of the greatest values of therapy is the experience of positive support. Although, we are trained in many therapeutic modalities, it is necessary to approach each Patient as though we are creating a new therapy uniquely for them. This begins with empathy and embracing the thought process of the Patient. Be mindful of the therapeutic relationship and how we regard each other.

Keep it simple. Don't highlight the diagnosis more than you highlight the symptoms. Prioritize that each of the Patient's experiences need to be fully seen and fully understood. Through this process you are able to identify remedies that are realistic. Avoid generalizing, at one session depression may be primary while at the next anxiety or mood instability. Begin each session as the Patient presents. And, close each session with reviewing their capabilities.

Encourage the Patient to plan as if it takes small steps to recover one's self. Embrace the process over worries about progress. Mutually monitor triggers to disruption in coping or setbacks. Listen to present stressors. Be a partner in treatment planning. Don't rush the outcome, don't problem solve, collaborate instead. Strive in each session to maintain a good place.

Pay close attention when you feel a Patient's mood is shifting. Discuss your concerns. If you voice your fears, it allows the Patient to be more open with theirs. Incorporate what you know from previous sessions. Identify new themes, work through them, move to other issues but maintain consistency to deepen perspective. Establish that you can shift to meet their changing needs including time of crisis.

Seek advice, collaborate with other treatment providers. Authentically state your viewpoint as it represents the Patient's viewpoint as well. Learn from your mistakes and always keep the Patient informed of them. Advocate. Make follow up phone calls when you feel it is necessary. Have insight to their psychosocial stressors. It is difficult for anyone to function under increased personal stress.

Explore with your Patient. Help them to let go of self-defeating patterns and feel differently. Use the sessions as a practice run for what they want to achieve. Recognize and use your healing capabilities. And always thrive for growth in each therapeutic session.

-Shannon Murphy, LPC, CPCS

# APPENDIX G

## When I Woke Up

### By Ashley Smith

"Mommy, take your medicine and go to sleep," Big Boy said in his small voice as his little hands raced miniature cars in the air at my bedside. Immediately, I felt guilty. I failed him, and myself. My mother instilled high expectations that I struggled to meet. I shamefully dropped my head to mask the multitude of ill feelings buried within. All I could do was turn my head to escape my reality.

My reality was that my four-year-old child unknowingly articulated my depressive state. He expressed my dilemma of depression without thought or understanding of the meaning of his statement. My small child's words were a double-edged sword that punctured my core, opened my eyes, and broke me down further. Before this event. I did not identify my depression as another obstacle to parenting. However, it was.

I had to learn to accept my condition and to manage it better in order to lift my head up and match the image of the "good mother" that my own mother had so strongly instilled in me. Depression attacked self-confidence that stirred up guilt, shame, and a negative perspective about my past, current, and ability to parent.

More often than not, I struggled with low energy, anxiety, and tiredness. These symptoms were an ongoing battle that challenged my physical, emotional, and psychological being. I struggled with our daily routine and demands. Whenever we returned home, I planned to clean the kitchen, cook a full meal, however, that task demanded energy, energy that I did not have most days. Thankfully, Big Boy loved chicken nuggets, fries, and fruit; I heated the nuggets and fries, opting for fruit instead of vegetables in order to make quick meals for him. My strained energy level restricted endurance with ordinary tasks. Accordingly, my tired physique landed me in bed more than usual.

It was challenging to discipline my son during my worst days with depression; I lacked the energy to enforce rules. However, depression came and went throughout the day and weeks, and sometimes we had great moments over typical day-to-day challenges - in spite of my depression.

I remember an incident with my son that boosted my self-confidence as a single-parent and reinforced the fact that I can live up to the expectations and standards that my mother instilled in me. It was on a Saturday, and I had to go to the bank at a busy time for other people, as well. As we know, banks close early on Saturdays and generally do not have public restrooms.

Big Boy and I were seated in the overcrowded bank lobby. Suddenly, he kicked the coffee table, pushed off the signage, and grabbed my cell phone then threw it to the floor! We got the attention of the entire crowd of the small bank, and there was no restroom for a pep talk, spanking, or proper scolding.

Fortunately, advice from friends and family immediately came to mind — and into play. I couldn't tolerate his behavior (neither could the crowd), but I could not leave! The bank was minutes from closing and locking us in until we finished our business. I had to act quick! I managed as best I could in front of our audience from the seat of the lobby chair.

I grabbed my four-year-old son, put him over my lap with an undeniable quickness, and spanked him. Then my cell phone rang. I picked my cell phone off the floor, answered the call, and abruptly ended the conversation, placing the phone back on the floor. I maintained a firm tone and ordered my son to clean up the mess he made. "You better clean this mess up exactly how you found it!" I calmly, and firmly instructed him.

He screamed and wrestled with me, but I did not let him go or get out of my seat. The bank manager encouraged me to step into a nearby office because he would not stop screaming. I respectfully declined and focused on guiding his small body in the direction where I pointed for him to pick up everything.

Afterwards, a man approached me with a religious pamphlet and complimented me for disciplining my son "with dignity." Eventually, I was in line again. The bank teller was also the bank manager who had encouraged me to take my son into the office to quiet him, and she complimented me too. Now, every time I visited that banking location, she remembers me and asks about my son!

While that may seem like a typical single-parent situation, it boosted my self-esteem booster, reminding me that I *can* manage. It was clear to me that I must take back control over my life and win this war on depression in order to be the parent I needed to be for Big Boy – and myself.

Over the next couple of years, I fought against my symptoms of depression. Finally, I told my doctor, "I want to get back on anti-depressants." Requesting anti-depressants was evidence of extensive growth in recovery. A few weeks after starting this medication I felt like a thick cloud of fog lifted and I finally woke up. Literally, my thought-processes cleared, and my memory sharpened, along with my motor skills.

My days with anxiety became almost non-existent! The combination of my schizophrenia and depression medications enhanced my energy, minimized my oversleeping, and quickly stabilized my motivation and self-confidence. I had more energy and focus to complete day-to-day routines at work and home in order to interact with my son the way that I wanted to.

Having depression does not have to take away the essence of being a good parent or employee. Through experience, I learned to practice the skills necessary to be the parent I aim to be. Trust, acceptance, and communication with my doctor helps me to practice self-care, be a good role model of recovery, and to be a better parent. I came a long way in my recovery with depression and schizophrenia. Practicing good self-care through acceptance and communication with my doctor enabled me to get back to having more fun, being able to manage his tantrums while spending more quality time with my son.

Treatment, awareness, and communication enabled me to have more energy and fun, to engage more with Big Boy, and secure my livelihood. As my son matures, I realize that managing my treatment is like disciplining my son. Discipline requires attention, support, and proper tools to manage effectively. However, there will be challenges and setbacks, which is a part of life's stresses. There will be good days, and bad days, however, I accept that treatment allows me to be the parent I strive to be, which is more like my mother. This requires work. I am disciplining my diagnoses, and I know that peers in recovery can too!

# LINKS AND RESOURCES

❖ **Ashley's Blog, Overcoming Schizophrenia**

Personal blog about Ashley's recovery journey that offers hope and awareness.

      o Website: http://overcomingschizophrenia.blogspot.com

      o Email: see website

❖ **Appalachian Consulting Group (ACG)**

The Appalachian Consulting Group trains and consults in health and behavioral health to promote a national workforce of peer specialists who call forth the potential within each individual to self-manage a healthy life with meaning and purpose.

      o Website: http://acgpeersupport.com/

      o Email: info@acgpeersupport.com

❖ **Better Help**

Making professional counseling accessible, affordable, convenient - so anyone who struggles with life's challenges can get help, anytime, anywhere.

      o Website: https://www.betterhelp.com

      o Email: contact@betterhelp.com

❖ **Brian and Behavior Research Foundation**

The Brain & Behavior Research Foundation is committed to alleviating the suffering caused by mental illness by awarding grants that will lead to advances and breakthroughs in scientific research.

  ○ Website: https://www.bbrfoundation.org

  ○ Email: info@bbrfoundation.org

❖ **Champions of Science: The Art of Ending Stigma**

The Art of Ending Stigma is a global project aimed at enhancing the conversation about eliminating stigma while calling out the importance of scientific insights about mental illnesses. Through public engagement, the program will encourage people to demonstrate how art, in its many forms, can help transcend mental illnesses and lead to a better understanding of them.

  ○ Website: http://artofendingstigma.com/

  ○ Email: see website

❖ **Copeland Center for Wellness and Recovery**

The mission of the Copeland Center for Wellness and Recovery is to promote personal, organizational, and community wellness and empowerment. We focus on shifting the system of mental health care toward a prevention and recovery focus. As the system shifts to reform through education, training, and research, we use the accomplishments developed and implemented by the people being served and the people who care for them. We reinforce this by building networks that reflect mutual support and community organizational empowerment.

o Website https://copelandcenter.com

o Email: info@copelandcenter.com

## ❖ CURESZ Foundation

To support a multifaceted educational campaign to correct the misperceptions about schizophrenia among the general public, using multiple media platforms. To provide education about cutting edge and underutilized medications and treatments and feature stories of hope.

o Website: https://curesz.org

o Email: bethany.yeiser@curesz.org

## ❖ Depression and Bipolar Support Alliance (DBSA)

DBSA provides hope, help, support, and education to improve the lives of people who have mood disorders.

o Website https://www.dbsalliance.org

o Email: See Website

## ❖ Georgia Mental Health Consumer Network (GMHCN)

The mission of the Georgia Mental Health Consumer Network is to promote recovery through advocacy, education, employment, empowerment, peer support, and self-help, and to unite as one voice to support the priorities set each year at the annual statewide peer conference.

o Website: https://www.gmhcn.org

o Email: info@gmhcn.org

❖ **Health Central—Schizophrenia**

The latest research and trends in schizophrenia, including promising treatments and ways to manage the disorder. Patient experts inspire with their testimonials of hope.

  o Website:

  https://www.healthcentral.com/category/schizophrenia

  o Email: See website

❖ **Hearing Voices Network (HVN)**

We focus on helping to create respectful and empowering spaces, whilst challenging the inequalities and oppressive practices that hold people back.

  o Website: http://www.hearing-voices.org

  o Email: info@hearing-voices.org

❖ **Mental Health America**

Mental Health America (MHA) - founded in 1909 - is the nation's leading community-based nonprofit dedicated to addressing the needs of those living with mental illness and to promoting the overall mental health of all Americans. Our work is driven by our commitment to promote mental health as a critical part of overall wellness, including prevention services for all; early identification and intervention for those at risk; integrated care, services, and supports for those who need it; with recovery as the goal.

  o Website: https://www.mhanational.org/4mind4body

  o Email: see website

❖ **National Alliance on Mental Illness (NAMI)**

NAMI, the National Alliance on Mental Illness, is the nation's largest grassroots mental health organization dedicated to building better lives for the millions of Americans affected by mental illness.

- o Website: https://nami.org

- o Email: info@nami.org

❖ **National Institute of Mental Health (NIMH)**

The National Institute of Mental Health (NIMH) is the lead federal agency for research on mental disorders.

- o Website: https://www.nami.org

- o Email: nimhinfo@nih.gov

❖ **National Institutes of Health (NIH)**

The National Institutes of Health (NIH), a part of the U.S. Department of Health and Human Services, is the nation's medical research agency — making important discoveries that improve health and save lives.

- o Website: https://www.nih.gov

- o Email: see website

❖ **National Resource Center on Psychiatric Advance Directives**

Psychiatric advance directives are relatively new legal instruments that may be used to document a competent person's specific instructions or preferences regarding future mental health treatment. Psychiatric advance directives can be used to plan for the possibility that someone may lose capacity to give or withhold informed consent to treatment during acute episodes of psychiatric illness.

- o Website: https://www.nrc-pad.org

- o Email: see website

❖ **Rethink Mental Illness**

We improve the lives of people severely affected by mental illness through our network of local groups and services, expert information and successful campaigning. Our goal is to make sure everyone affected by severe mental illness has a good quality of life.

- o Website: https://www.rethink.org

- o Email: see website

❖ **Schizophrenia.com**

Started in 1995, Schizophrenia.com is an internet community dedicated to providing high quality information, support and education to the family members, caregivers, and individuals whose lives have been impacted by schizophrenia.

- o Website: http://schizophrenia.com/

- o Email: szwebmaster@yahoo.com

❖ **Schizophrenia and Related Disorders Alliance of America (SARDAA)**

The Schizophrenia and Related Disorders Alliance of America promotes improvement in lives affected by schizophrenia-related brain illnesses (mental illnesses involving psychosis). SARDAA promotes hope and recovery through support programs, education, collaboration, and advocacy.

    o Website: https://sardaa.org

    o Email: info@sardaa.org

❖ **Schizophrenia Society of Nova Scotia (SSNS)**

The Schizophrenia Society of Nova Scotia (SSNS) works to improve the quality of life for those affected by schizophrenia, psychosis, bipolar and related mental disorders through education, support programs, influencing public policy, and encouraging research.

    o Website: http://www.ssns.ca/home.html

    o Email: contact@ssns.ca

❖ **Social Security Administration**

The mission of the Social Security Administration (SSA) is to administer national Social Security programs as prescribed by legislation in an equitable, effective, efficient, and caring manner.

    o Website: https://www.ssa.gov

    o Email: see website

❖ **Substance Abuse and Mental Health Services Administration (SAMHSA)**

SAMHSA's mission is to reduce the impact of substance abuse and mental illness on America's communities.

o Website: https://www.samhsa.gov

o Email: see website

❖ **Suicide Prevention Lifeline**

The Lifeline provides 24/7, free and confidential support for people in distress, prevention, and crisis resources.

o Website: https://suicidepreventionlifeline.org

o 1-800-273-TALK [8255]

❖ **Wellness Recovery Action Plan (WRAP)**

The Wellness Recovery Action Plan or WRAP, is a self-designed prevention and wellness tool that you can use to get well, and stay well. WRAP is for anyone, any time, and for any of life's challenges

o Website: https://mentalhealthrecovery.com

o Email:info@WRAPandRecoveryBooks.com

[This Page is Blank Intentionally for Notes]

[This Page is Blank Intentionally for Notes]

[This Page is Blank Intentionally for Notes]

[This Page is Blank Intentionally for Notes]

[This Page is Blank Intentionally for Notes]

[This Page is Blank Intentionally for Notes]

# ABOUT THE AUTHOR

Ashley Smith is a mental health advocate, speaker, and mother. Since 2008, Ashley has been sharing her recovery story on her blog, *Overcoming Schizophrenia*. For over ten years, Ashley has maintained her blog, remaining open about her recovery journey. She aims to offer hope and awareness through her blog.

Her recovery experience was one of three stories depicted in the documentary, Living with Schizophrenia: A Call for Hope and Recovery (Janssen Pharmaceuticals, 2011). In 2014, Ashley self-published her first book, *What's On My Mind? A Collection of Blog Entries from Overcoming Schizophrenia*. Ashley is a former board member and state trainer for NAMI Georgia, Inc. She is also a trained speaker with the Respect Institute of Georgia.

Currently, Ashley is a part of the CURESZ Foundation Advisory Council, an organization that focuses on awareness. Ashley is passionate about mental health advocacy, parenting her son, Big Boy, and living a quality life in recovery.

Ashley resides in Atlanta, Georgia and maintains her blog, *Overcoming Schizophrenia*. To learn more about Ashley Smith, visit her blog at overcomingschizophrenia.blogspot.com.

**Also by Ashley Smith**

# WHAT'S ON MY MIND?

## A Collection of Blog Entries from

## Overcoming Schizophrenia

**Volume I**

**Foreword by Christina Bruni**

**Available on Amazon**

**What readers said:**

"I can't put it down. What a powerful testimony..." –Francis W.

"Before reading your book, I didn't even know there were treatment options available... I just want to thank you for shedding light on a subject that is quite uncomfortable to talk about." –Roman N.

"You captured my awareness by the way you expressed yourself of what you have been through." –Ryan R.

Made in the USA
Columbia, SC
28 January 2020